Finding My Voice:
Standing Against Racism

W. Nadine White

This book is a memoir. It depicts actual events in the author's life as truthfully as recollections permit. All persons within are real individuals. The locations and names of some individuals have been changed to respect their privacy.

Finding My Voice: Standing Against Racism
Copyright © 2023 by W. Nadine White
Illustration © 2023 by Alyssa Lasko
Design © 2023 by Chakib Azzaoui

All rights reserved. No part of this publication may be reproduced, except for the use of excerpts in a book review, educational, or business purposes. Please contact W. Nadine White at nadinewhitemediation.com for further information regarding permission.

Published by Mediation-Ability Press
Library and Archives Canada

ISBN:978-1-7782709-9-4(eBook)
ISBN:978-1-7782709-8-7(Paperback)

First Edition: 2023

To two extraordinary persons:
my mother, Hazel Powell,
and
my best friend, Calvin Samuels

Contents

Preface 7

Chapter 1: The Beginning 9

Chapter 2: Hostile Environment 13

Chapter 3: A Fresh Start 39

Chapter 4: Turning Point 47

Chapter 5: Pressured But Not Crushed 51

Chapter 6: Father Passing 59

Chapter 7: Obstacles Into Opportunities 69

Chapter 8: Staying Afloat 77

Chapter 9: What Happened Next 85

Chapter 10: A Spiritual Encounter 91

Chapter 11: Next Act 101

Chapter 12: God Answers Prayer 113

Chapter 13: The Replacement 125

Chapter 14: My Identity 129

Chapter 15: Moving Forward 137

Chapter 16: Reflection 143

Acknowledgments 144

About the Author 145

Preface

This book is a culmination of many years of coping with the unending adversities of racial discrimination in the workplace. Being a Black woman in Canada, I experienced the rooted racism and oppression inherent in our institutions and colleagues who knew of my struggles with prejudice but discounted my experiences. Those times were often daunting and isolating, but I recognized that my inner strength came from God.

I discovered the person I want to become through my journey and how to choose peace instead of unleashing anger. I decided to change my thoughts from negative to positive, focus on my emotional healing, and choose to love myself and forgive others.

In sharing my experiences with several individuals who supported me then and continue to do so today, I recognized the profound impact their perspectives of life's challenges had on me. My progressive friends from different ethnic backgrounds acknowledged their privileges and understood my plight and marginalization in the organization. For that, I am grateful.

Nadine White

Chapter 1
The Beginning

"Wow!" I can remember saying this soon after I read the acceptance letter from Centennial College. "Incredible!"

In truth, my feelings were more like, *Is this real? I can't believe it's happening!*

It was enthusiasm, mixed with a bit of apprehension. I wanted a change. The work I was doing at the time had become monotonous and less exciting, and I realized the full-time job, dental, health benefits, and profit sharing at Novopharm would soon end. Also, I understood if I was indeed going to pursue my dreams, I had to take a chance, and where I was, there was no opportunity for promotion. I would be stuck in the quality control department as a data entry clerk, doing the same thing every day.

Night school was my only option to acquire my grade twelve English credit for college admission. During the wintry nights, I waited for the buses. The wind whipped through the trees, creaking, and groaning like an old farmhouse.

Another letter arrived in the mail from Centennial after my resignation. I would need to pass a math test before the semester started. I panicked. What if I failed? Would I still be enrolled in the program? I had already quit and had no job. I embraced that in my life as a single twenty-three-year-old woman; I would have to take risks to attain my goal.

But when I walked into the exam room that muggy afternoon, my self-confidence proved I would pass the test. Days before the classes began, I got a congratulatory letter that confirmed my acceptance into the three-year business administration program.

I phoned my tutor and told him the great news. I was ecstatic, as I would be the first among my siblings to attend college.

Months later, in February 1991, I accepted a part-time receptionist position at Bluefale Acres Long-term Care Nursing Home, City of Toronto. Bluefale Acres was a busy home nestled beside a general hospital. I managed multiple telephone calls, directed paramedics to the floors, and helped with emergencies. After hectic days, by 6:00 p.m., the first floor was quiet, allowing me time to study.

We worked as a cohesive team and fostered a favorable climate. Lorette, who was Black, wore her hair up in a ponytail. She mostly worked the day shift. April, also Black, studied accounting in her downtime. Edith, a senior white clerk with a British accent, assigned most of our tasks. Eliana, a Jewish administrator, spoke with a gentle voice.

Two years later, things changed as people came and went. Eliana transferred to another location, and new administrators, team members, and people with different leadership styles came. Lorette left to work at a private school, and April moved back to Antigua after university. Edith had a promotion to a position at the head office.

Shier, a white administrator, walked with a limp and took deep breaths between every sentence. Caty, her assistant, was Italian, short in stature, and strode quickly across the floor when walking through the lobby.

The atmosphere in the office shifted, and collaboration ceased. The earlier years when I started at Bluefale Acres were now memories, and I wished they would come back again.

Chapter 2
Hostile Environment

Despite having a business administration college diploma and pursuing a degree in the same field, I knew what it felt like to be overlooked. For the last five years, administrators had me train white employees with less education, seniority, and experience for the same jobs I didn't get. Instead, they cross-trained Filipinos and whites in other departments, but there were no prospects of advancement for me, a qualified Black woman.

On November 18, 1994, I wrote to the general manager.

Dear Mr. Coley,

This letter explained our telephone conversation yesterday and why I feel Caty and Shier are discriminating against me, because I am Black.

My hours each week decreased to eighteen hours for unspecified reasons. Caty told me, "I'm not obligated to do call-ins by seniority, and I can call whom I choose." A white housekeeper and a Filipino dietary-aid staff trained to fill the full-time position I had applied for in administration.

It is challenging to cope with daily monitoring. I arrived two minutes after my shift started because of a motor vehicle accident, and the bus had rerouted.

Instead of understanding that the situation was out of my control, Caty raised her eyebrows and said, "Why are you late? One bad erase all the good."

Mr. Coley, the unfair treatment has been affecting me emotionally. She is not evaluating me based on my performance or ability but on my skin color.

I intended to file a complaint with the Human Rights Commission. However, having spoken to you, I am convinced with your help, you can resolve this matter without their involvement. I do not believe this is how the City of Toronto wants to treat its employees when it is against discrimination and striving for equality.

Nadine White

I filed grievances and had various meetings, but the inequity intensified. In January 1995, the union rep sent another letter to the general manager and a copy of the schedules.

Dear Mr. Coley,

Please note that the dietary-aid staff has been working most Mondays, Wednesdays, and Thursdays 7 hours at reception. She canceled her shifts to work in administration. They neglected to enter them on the schedule. As you can see, this is unfair and unequal treatment toward Nadine.

Sincerely,

Steward

Caty left Bluefale Acres after the city denied her another employment contract.

When I thought things would improve, they got worse. Shier told me at the interview feedback for a purchasing clerk post, "You're not suitable for the job. You're not good at anything." Those hurtful words sunk deep inside me.

Days turned into weeks, and my head pounded. I couldn't open my eyes. The visits to the doctor became a weekly routine. I had no choice but to stay in bed, away from noises and bright lights.

My shift began at 8:30 in the morning. I dressed, ate breakfast, took a migraine medication, and got ready for work. I threw on my hat, jacket, scarf, and gloves. I hurried to catch the bus. I exited at the rear at the stop, walking on the snowy sidewalk to the entrance.

It was March 6, 1998, and the snow sparkled with ice crystals, freshly fallen snowflakes bouncing on the top whenever a breeze stirred the air. Sitting at the reception desk, the reflection of the sunlight through the skylights brightened the area.

Residents lounged around the warm fire, reading magazines, and relaxing in the spacious, enormous lobby with a two-sided fireplace. Elvis Presley played in the background.

Seconds later, I glanced at the view outside the huge glass window and pondered my goals. I was a young, vibrant Black woman with dreams and aspirations to pursue a career in the government. Those dreams had shattered after working seven years part-time and being denied several full-time job opportunities.

After getting a cup of peppermint tea, I returned to my desk. I heard Jezebella Foote's loud voice echoing from a distance. She was a white middle-class Canadian employed at Bluefale Acres as a personal support worker since 1975. Her workplace accidents in nursing had landed her a job in the office.

Jezebella was known to be both divisive and contentious. She strategized, executed, and attacked to ignite arguments she knew would trigger adverse reactions.

She approached me at the reception desk, glaring. "Do you have the telephone receipt?"

"No."

She disappeared and returned fifteen minutes later. "NADINE, AREN'T YOU GOING TO GIVE ME THE RECEIPT?"

She startled me. I hesitated to respond.

Her voice raised to a sharp shrill. "I don't know why you're working here."

Stunned, I rushed into the office to speak with Nancita, the white assistant administrator. She sat alone in the boardroom, flipping through papers with her hair tucked behind her ears.

"Excuse me, Nancita. I want to talk with you before I leave for home."

Without eye contact, she said, "What's it regarding?"

"Jezebella."

"Document the incident."

"OK, I will."

This was her typical response, and nothing ever changed.

I strolled to my desk, and Jezebella followed me, spewing racial slurs. "You Black b*tch. You're worthless. I'm going to get you out of here for good."

I tried re-entering the office, but Jezebella braced her back against the entrance and barred me from going through the doors. I squeezed through a small gap and stomped inside. She walked behind me, removed her eyeglasses, and pushed into my space. I extended my arm and yelled, "Leave me alone! You called me a "black b*tch!"

My finger unintentionally brushed against her face.

Nancita screeched. "What's going on?"

I tried to explain, but she thundered, "Nadine, take your things and go home! Don't return until you hear from us!"

Tears gushed down my face as I left the building in shame. The drive home on the bus felt longer than usual, plagued by thoughts of injustice, and lies being told about me.

Over two years of harassment, abuse, and threats, and now they want to have me fired, but they did nothing to stop her; because I'm Black.

I opened my door. Mama was perplexed. "What

are you doing home so early? Not the migraine headache."

I leaned against the wall, rubbing my eyes, "Jezebella again. Worse this time."

"Lord, Jesus! What's wrong with that woman?"

"I did everything to avoid her."

"What's the supervisor doing about it?"

"Not sure. Mama, she always gets her way."

"Sit down. Don't worry."

"No one cares. I'm tired of Jezebella's confrontations."

Mama removed the golden-brown Jamaican beef patties from the oven. She put one on my plate. "Eat. Don't starve yourself."

"Thanks, but I'm not hungry."

Leaving my snack on the kitchen counter, I strolled downstairs to the basement, thinking how much things had changed in the last two years. I once had a bright future, but it was over. I lay on the red carpet in the dark room, snuggled underneath my pink blanket, and tears gushed onto the cushion.

A few days passed, and I didn't hear from Nancita regarding the altercation with Jezebella. Two weeks later, a courier delivered the disciplinary letter from Bluefale Acres. "Neither your verbal nor the written account [are] consistent with the action I observed. This confirms a two-month suspension without pay. Your return to work depends on enrollment in an Anger Management course approved by our

Employee Assistance Program."

I stared at the letter and wept; both hands covered my face.

Mama touched her mouth. "What happened?"

"I'm suspended for two months. No income."

"How about the troublemaker?"

"Not sure."

"Are you worried about the money? I'll work overtime to cover the bills."

"I'm confused. I can't think."

Hazel, my mother, worked at Novopharm as a packaging operator. She spoke in a whisper and seemed younger than her age. Her sixty-eighth birthday was in four months, but she never considered retirement.

We lived in a four-bedroom townhouse in an urban area, the northeast end of the City of Toronto. Together, we paid the mortgage, utility, land taxes, and basic amenities——a considerable weight to handle on her own.

I found myself a devastated thirty-year-old single woman, heartbroken after my mother had to work overtime to shoulder the entire household expenses. I hadn't signed up for this when I moved to Canada. There were endless opportunities, but it was a struggle for a Black woman to attain her full potential.

The long spell of cold days ended. I peeped through the kitchen window, in the backyard, and reminisced on the Jamaican motto. "Out of Many, One People" which symbolizes the distinct cultures that came together as a nation. Our multiculturalism embraced diversity on the island. Partisan, colorism and socio-economic problems existed, but hate crime due to people's skin color was discouraged or non-existent.

I was amused and captivated by the diverse culture when I arrived in Canada. Soon, I realized Canadian's reputation as polite was a myth to conceal their arrogance and anti-Black racism.

Many days passed in a blur. Yet, my mind drifted to registering for the anger management course at Clarke's Institute of Psychiatry as a requirement for returning to work.

Finally, I registered and received pages of a questionnaire in the mail along with a pamphlet. I scanned it, my heart hammering in my chest. "The Clinic serves perpetrators of violence to prevent the expression of anger as violent behavior. . . Adult males with a history of repeated impulsive aggressive behavior directed towards other persons."

I let out a quick bark of laughter, and a heaviness descended in my stomach as I collapsed to the floor.

Calvin, my best friend, rang the doorbell, but I couldn't get up to answer. He let himself in with the spare key I gave him in case of an emergency.

I lay at the edge of the bed with my head propped high on the pillow. The beige vertical fabric blinds remained closed at the slide doors to a walk-out balcony, preventing the light inside.

Calvin walked in and shook me. "Wake up. What's the matter?"

In a faint voice, I said, "Read this."

He rubbed his bald head and said, "She wants to destroy you. You need your strength if you want to win."

"There's none left."

We talked briefly, and he went home after my mother came from work.

My girlfriend, Sandi, quoted the Psalms at night before I fell asleep. She read with a quiet and pleasant tone. Nie, an acquaintance, checked in daily and sometimes fetched me lunch. Mama's fervent prayers and encouragement never failed. These supports were comforting in my worst anxieties.

I mailed the completed questionnaire to Clarke's Institute and awaited their reply.

A call came from a private number. "May I speak with Nadine White?" She had a soft voice. People were chatting and chuckling in the background.

"Speaking."

"How are you doing today?"

"I'm fine."

"This is the officer . . . From 41 Division. Your coworker, Jezebella Foote, filed an assault against you. Please report to the station."

"When would you like me to?"

"As soon as possible."

That early afternoon, after I hung up the phone, I gazed into the bedroom closet mirror and pictured the police handcuffing me and throwing me into jail. My lips trembled with watery eyes.

I rang Calvin immediately. "I need to go to the police station."

"Why?"

"Jezebella laid charges, but I'm unsure of the details."

"I'll take you."

I paced the floor; Jezebella's words kept sounding in my ear. "I'm going to get you out of here." It was now clear what she meant. Why would she go to such an extent when she instigated everything? The altercation was on March 6, almost two months before, and now she was pressing charges. What were her motives?

After arriving at the police station, I gave my name to a well-dressed officer in a dark blue uniform who manned a small window. I had never been incarcerated or arrested, and I was nervous. A sudden throbbing pain began in my head.

The man offered me a quick half-smile and motioned me to sit in the chair. "Please roll your fingertips in ink, then press them on the card."

So, I did.

"Come with me. Face the camera before you."

He took several mugshots from different angles.

"You'll appear in court on Friday, June 12, 1998, at 2:00 p.m. Here is the information, along with the location and courtroom."

My headache sharpened, stabbing behind my eyes, and making me feel sick.

I gave a feeble grin. "Thank you."

When I got back to the car, Calvin switched on the engine. "Don't worry. I'll help you obtain a lawyer."

"I can't stop worrying. The police fingerprinted, photographed, and entered my profile in the criminal's database." Millions of thoughts ran through my mind.

Back in my bedroom, I rested on the light grey carpet, head on my knees with my back against the bed. "God, why can't you open the earth and let it swallow Jezebella alive? Make her disappear forever." I sobbed, wiping the tears with my hands, filled with hate. I gasped for air. "Father, please forgive me." I had never felt such hatred for another human, and I didn't want it to consume me.

A devoted Pentecostal Christian, the bible says to love my enemies. Only I realized how hard it is to follow this precept while facing a criminal record and possible jail time.

Meanwhile, Clarke's Institute offered the option of an anger management group closer to home.

I met with Bondi Ambrims, a mental health professional at Centenary Hospital. She was cordial. Her office was on the sixth floor. After the two-hour intake interview, she told me, "You don't belong in this program . . . Since workplace stress contributed to the recent incident, you might benefit from a stress management group coping with workplace stressors. With your consent, I'll inform your supervisor."

Bondi phoned Nancita. After she hung up, she said, "Your supervisor has set you up. She is outraged you're here and only approved the Clarke Institute. That's where she wants you to go. Don't worry; I'll write you a letter with my recommendations. I've never done this before, but it's a risk I'm willing to take."

We shook hands. "Thank you very much!" I said.

She wrote, "In the absence of problems with overtly aggressive displays of anger, Ms. White would probably not benefit from attending our anger management group . . . She might also benefit from acquiring enhanced communication skills, especially those concerned with expressing negative feelings. Individual counseling might be more suitable in this last respect."

"I informed her supervisor of my conclusions and my recommendations. After what she believed was only a one-hour assessment session (two hours), her supervisor suggested I had insufficient information to make any treatment recommendations. She informed me that only her treatment at the Clarke Institute would be acceptable. I understand the Clarke Institute only accepts men for treatment in their anger groups."

I left dumbfounded. Wow, I couldn't believe Bondi did that for me. A white person!

The notion popped into my head soon after I walked inside the elevator. White colleagues and supervisors showed empathy but dismissed my experiences and avoided me. I was always on guard because I didn't trust white people. Bondi was no different in my mind until she performed a selfless act.

Clarke's Institute of Psychiatry was for men with a history of impulsive behaviors. Nancita demanded I attend their program, although I didn't fit the profile or express any resentment in an overtly violent way when mistreated. The City of Toronto intended to have me jailed, a scheme to build their case and grounds for dismissal.

Incarcerating an aggressive Black woman would be the perfect solution to block me from future employment with government institutions and well-established organizations, leaving me only a passport to underpaid jobs without benefits and protection.

On the morning of the hearing, I met with my lawyer, and we went over the charges Jezebella brought against me. I was oblivious to the details until I read the prosecutor's information.

Jezebella wrote, "Nadine head-butted me with her forehead on my left forehead." Nancita wrote, "Nadine punched Jezebella's right cheek." The police report read, "Striking the victim on the face . . . she suffered a swollen right side with a slight bump on her forehead."

I was outraged at the injustice and blamed for everything.

Afterward, Calvin ordered me pizza. I couldn't eat much. I was too numb. "You're going to be okay. Trust God." I tried to believe his thoughtful and comforting words.

Mama fell asleep. I tossed and turned in bed, considering the day's events and the upcoming psychiatrist appointment. My life was in ruins. I faced a possible conviction, paying expensive legal costs, not working, and seeing a therapist. I didn't envision this insanity in my life.

It was an hour-and-a-half ride on the bus and train from home to Clarke's Institute in Toronto. Upon arrival, I checked in at the front desk and waited a few minutes. Doctor Santra, the psychiatrist, a tall young Indian man, greeted me in the waiting area.

"Come with me, Nadine."

I stepped into his well-lit office with a street view and glanced through the window, where I saw high-rise buildings and people strolling across the street.

"Please have a seat."

"Thanks."

"How are you today?"

"Fine."

Initially, I was apprehensive, but my anxiety diminished after his introduction. "Here," I said. "Bondi Ambrims from Centenary Hospital's Anger Management group wanted me to give you this letter."

He read it right away. "Well, this is a start. We will focus our sessions on dealing with stress and coping strategies. Can we meet twice a week?"

"Yes."

I left the first session with a glimmer of hope. His words resonated with me. "Deal with the things in your control and leave the rest to the expert." We spoke about everyday challenges in many of those sessions, and I was eager for the next meeting. I was thinking, *not bad at all. What's thrown at me with evil intent, God will turn into something staggering.*

As the final hours approached, fear gripped my soul. *But I must go back to work if I want to win.*

My gut twisted as I shuffled into the office after the two months suspension. I organized backlog files in the dark corner with a dimmed ceiling light from 11:00 a.m. to 1:00 p.m. daily. It was a new job with reduced hours, isolated from human interactions, and under heightened scrutiny. One thing that kept me going and calm was listening to *CHFI 98.1 FM* on an antique radio. Some of my favourite artists were Toni Braxton, Celine Dion, Mariah Carey, Bob Marley, and Michael Jackson.

Mr. Wicker was my first lawyer for the upcoming court hearing, and he arrived late for our first court appearance and proved impossible to contact. Now he was missing in action.

I was scrambling to find another lawyer before the January 5, 1999 trial, and finally retained one after various attempts. He was Scottish and professional. The judge rescheduled the hearing until he was familiar with the case.

My attorney convinced me the judge would drop the charge. He noted that Jezebella and the witness fabricated their statements. It was the pinch of optimism I needed to trust the judicial system.

In the meantime, I mailed a letter to the Law Society for full reimbursement and received $1,200 in compensation, three hundred dollars less than I anticipated. Not that I was complaining. At least he showed up.

During our brief hearing, my lawyer argued the inconsistencies and referred to the two months of suspension I had already completed. He also said, "Nadine has no past criminal record. Your Honor, I'm asking the court to issue a peace bond." Without any hesitation, the judge granted his request and averted a trial.

The judge's handwritten note on the yellow 'RECOGNIZANCE TO KEEP THE PEACE' form read: "No contact directly or indirectly with Jezebella Foote. You will not be at Bluefale Acres while Jezebella Foote is on shift. It may be done through counsel if you require communication with Jezebella." It was signed and dated June 10, 1999.

I was pleased about breaking the pattern of a Black woman being incarcerated based on a White woman's lies. I found myself thinking. I'm *free once more. I don't have to deal with her ever again.*

Jezebella and Nancita hung their heads while making a hasty exit.

Not being charged with assault was crucial if I was to file complaints for unjust suspension, racial discrimination, and unfair treatment. After all, the City of Toronto promoted equal employment opportunities as outlined in its handbook and claimed, "A commitment to confront workplace harassment by a coworker to another . . . Unwelcome remarks about a person's color."

It seemed to me they had only created these

policies for optics as a deterrent to cover up racism and discrimination. Once I asked them to stand by their policies, the city labeled me as the offender. They deemed me an aggressive, loud, and angry Black Woman, stereotypes that had plagued me for many years in Canada.

Shier had been away from her desk during the issuance of the grievances. When she returned, she read the steward's grievances and darted from her office to where I filed residents' records. She was fuming and held the documents toward my face. "What is this? The dates are wrong."

I was shaking while I extended my right hand to accept the document. Shier pulled it back angrily. "You twisted my finger. Leave the building, now."

Powerless and distraught, I phoned Calvin for advice. He said, "Try to get home safely. We'll talk after work."

Nine days later, a courier delivered mail from Bluefale Acres. "You were on notice . . . a final warning, and that any further incident would result in termination . . . Effective immediately, your employment is terminated."

A sudden dread hit my core. I had nothing left in me—No tears. No energy. No solace, not even in the church.

Sandi read scriptures to me every night before I slept, and I meditated on them to keep me sane on many hard days.

Ps. 27 says, "The LORD is my light and my salvation; whom shall I fear? The LORD is the strength of my life; of whom shall I be afraid? When the wicked, even my enemies and foes, came upon me to eat up my flesh, they stumbled and fell. Although the host should encamp against me, my heart shall not fear. Though war should rise against me, I will remain confident. For in the time of trouble he shall hide me in his pavilion: in the secret of his tabernacle shall he hide me; and set me up upon a rock. Wait on the LORD: be of good courage, and he shall strengthen your heart: wait, I say, on the LORD."

Ps. 37 says, "Fret not yourself because of evildoers, neither envy the workers of iniquity, for they shall soon be cut down like the grass and wither as the green herb. The LORD orders the steps of a good man: and he delighted in his way. Although he falls, he shall not completely cast down: for the LORD uphold him with his hand."

Nye was one of my friends. He touched my shoulder. "Don't give up, Nadine. File a complaint to Human Rights. Don't give them the victory."

I had outstanding grievances: January 14, 1998 (denied hours and cross-training), March 16, 1998 (harassment and suspension), and August 12, 1998 (termination). The union escalated them to arbitration.

On November 16, 1998, I filed a complaint to the Ontario Human Rights Commission.

Human Rights acknowledged my claim and pursued action against the City of Toronto. The arbitration hearing was in June of the following year. In the meantime, I continued counseling and focused on full-time studies at York University.

My grades soared despite the adversities; a twinkle of hope was on the horizon. Doctor Santra's endless reassurance helped. "I understand it's not easy, but you have immense strength. If you did nothing, you would always wonder, 'What if'? If you try and lose, you'll know you have done your best."

"But I'm up against the government."

"Yes, but you have the union, Human Rights, and me on your side."

"Thank you. I never thought of it that way."

Mama and I always had gifts under the tree at Christmas. This year, the dismissal from my job put a damper on my spirit and pocket. But our traditions didn't end. We attended the Christmas morning service and invited our family for the season's observance.

For breakfast, we had organic hot chocolate, fresh bread, fried fish, and seasonal fruits.

Mama cooked succulent roasted chicken, rice, vegetables, and sweet potato pudding for our dinner. Our celebration centered on storytelling and watching movies.

The holiday was behind me, and the new year was imminent. After several rejections of permanent positions, I underwent a complete transformation. I took stock of my life, where I was, and where I was going and tackled each day with inner wisdom.

Still, the situation was far from perfect. Without a job, I had no income. I attended university full-time and received support via the Ontario Student Assistant Program (OSAP), which was enough to pay my tuition and day-to-day expenses. I survived through my faith that the divinity would provide. Mama and my friend's contributions were my lifelines.

I learned early that education and knowledge were power, a belief ingrained in Jamaican culture. A three-year Business Administration College diploma was a precursor to a lifelong learning journey. In my third year at university, having attained management and human resources professional certificates, I felt prepared for the workforce. It was a chance to venture into the market and find the ideal job.

Late Wednesday morning, I walked by the Hudson Bay department store and beamed with delight when I saw my reflection in the mirror. Today wasn't a day to feel incompetent and inadequate; it was for me to recapture my self-confidence and poise. I had a short haircut with tight curls and a slim body. The eyes of men enthralled me as I strolled through the mall, a further reminder I was a strong and attractive Black woman and not the unmanageable savage I had been made out to be.

I recalled my birthday party in July 1997. I almost forgot how glamorous I was with a similar hairstyle but a bit longer and a floral silky purple dress with soft pink, yellow, green, and light beige colors, the skin above my knees stunning. The sheer, thin satin stocking with matching tan shoes complemented the outfit. A DJ played music from the mid-sixties, and I danced and twirled. I posed for the camera and laughed with thirty multi-color balloons in my hands, "Happy 30th Birthday."

Although it had been eight months before, the memories still played in my mind. The last time I'd felt happy was before the altercation at work.

There was tension in the air as I strode into the lobby for the June 25, 1999 hearing. Everyone was gaping as if they had just seen a phantom and gossiped among themselves. Trying to calm my crippling nerves, I took a long deep breath and walked into my designated room.

I greeted the CUPE team as I stepped into the bright, sun-lit square and spacious room.

"Hi!" I waved to the lawyer, and Katie, the union representative.

Katie arose from the dark brown sofa, strode across the room, and shook my hand. "Nadine, how are you?" Her short-layered brunette hair revealed her twinkled eyes.

"I'm doing fine."

"Please have a seat."

"Thank you."

"Let's go over the city's offer."

We explored the options thoroughly, but they were conditional on various factors: withdrawing the grievances and Human Rights complaint, and making no further claims against them, their officials, and employees.

The union vetoed the City of Toronto's only option to hire me to work at the men's prison. They offered me a job in the harshest working climate while positions sat empty in other, kinder divisions.

Had I accepted this job, my anxiety could eventually exacerbate into a severe nervous breakdown.

There were other considerations: If the arbitrator didn't rule in my favor, I would receive bad references and no job. If I won, I would have the same part-time job, people, stress, and trust issues. If I settled, I would have no job but could apply for full-time employment in the educational field or with other organizations, a clear record, and a neutral letter. I would maintain my mental health and have no future job prospects with the city.

After the lawyer and Katie discussed my options, I declared, "It's overwhelming. I want to consult with my family."

"Absolutely!" said Katie.

I left the room and made the call.

"Calvin, I'm overwhelmed. These are the options the union presented to me. I need your help to decide."

"It's a tough one."

"Why don't you settle?"

"This way, I can start my life over. Right?"

"Yes."

"All right. Talk to you soon."

When I strolled back, I gave the union my decision.

Ultimately, I settled for a standard employment letter, ten thousand dollars, and my dignity without monetary damages for pain and suffering.

An agreement between the Canadian Union of Public Employees and the City of Toronto stated,

"Whereas the Employer discharged an employee named Nadine White (Grievor) by letter dated August 17, 1998, ... The parties wish to resolve the grievances without prejudice and precedent basis. Therefore, the Employer, Union, and Grievor have agreed as follows:

(1) The Grievor's discharge shall be set aside, and she shall be considered resigned effective August 17, 1998. The employer will amend the records accordingly.

(2) The Employer shall pay the Grievor the sum of $10 000, less the necessary deductions required by law, such money to be paid on or before August 1, 1999.

(3) The Employer shall provide the Grievor with a letter stating, "This letter will confirm that Nadine White was employed as a Part-time Clerk 3 in our Homes for the Aged Division from February 1991 until August 17, 1998, when she resigned."

(4) This Agreement shall constitute a full and final settlement of all the grievances.

(5) The Grievor agrees to withdraw and or not proceed with the Human Rights complaint, immediately contact the Commission and request to withdraw.

(6) In consideration of the payment referred to in paragraph 2, the Grievor releases the Employer, its officers, officials, agents, and assigns from all claims, demands, grievances, complaints, actions, causes of action, and proceedings at any nature or kind, statutory or otherwise arising out of her employment

and termination."

It was signed and dated in Toronto on June 25, 1999.

As I walked out, it was bittersweet. The city pressured me to drop the Human Rights claim, used power and public money to advance their interests, and covered up their actions. Yet, I felt the load lifted from me. I had no job, but my mind was free from mental slavery—*freedom at last.*

Fourteen months ago, I started stress management and working on coping strategies with Doctor Santra. I continued seeing him until a week after the arbitration.

"Tell me all about the hearing, Nadine," he said.

"It's over . . ."

"How do you feel about the outcome?"

"Joyful, uncertain, and drained."

Doctor Santra's striped grey and dark blue shirt was tucked into his jeans, and he leaned forward in his chair. "You did well. You won! It will take time to heal. Endless possibilities are waiting for you."

His office wall had affirmation posters. I watched him as he turned around to me and said, "Nadine, the worst is behind you. Here's my card. Don't hesitate to contact me if you need to talk."

"Thank you for helping me navigate this difficult time."

"Take care." We shook hands.

I exhaled a sigh of relief, held my head high,

shoulders back, and promenaded through the hallway. It may have taken until the last session, but I found closure to five years of emotional anguish and racism.

Friends and family celebrated the victory and my new adventure with a dinner party. Mama roasted beef, mashed potatoes, mixed vegetables, rice, and red kidney beans, seasoned with organic coconut milk, savory cornmeal pudding for dessert, and fruit punch. Everyone encouraged me on my new journey.

"Thank you all for your support!" I told them.

In September, the morning dawned with blue skies, and drizzling rain began to fall and lasted a few minutes. The sun finally broke through the rolling clouds at 18 degrees Celsius temperature.

I was watering the lily and aloe vera plants in the living room. My cordless phone rang.

"Hello."

"Good morning!" said Calvin. "A principal is looking for a temporary secretary in one of the Greater Toronto School Boards. Are you interested?"

"Yes, please."

"The principal would like to interview you on Monday. You could start next week."

"Are you joking?"

"No."

"Thanks."

"No one is greater than you, God. You are amazing!"

Chapter 3
A Fresh Start

September 1999 gave way to a new start. The streak of bad luck seemed to be over. My career and life were about to align, and I was thrilled to work for the Greater Toronto Area School Board, standing in awe of its diversity, unique cultures, and ethnic groups.

Brownsflore Public School had a delightful atmosphere. I liked my time at work, had a sense of purpose, was respected, and flourished in positive workplace culture. The principal served the office staff tea in the afternoon. It was exceptional.

Everything was moving in the right direction until I received registered mail from employee services.

Dear Nadine White,

Our records indicate the police reference check has revealed information that requires clarification. One of the Greater Toronto School Board's Conditions of Employment is submitting proof of a satisfactory criminal record check, as stated on the application form you signed.

This letter is to confirm you have twenty (20) days from the date of this letter to make an appointment with the Superintendent of Employee Relations, Gentle Bliss, to review your Police Check. Summary.

Based on the information in the Summary, He will confirm or rescind your employment offer. You will not be eligible for future employment with the Board.

Sincerely,

Human Resources

This ghost from my past haunted me for weeks. *What did this mean for me?*

I counted myself fortunate the assault result on the police background check didn't justify an employment withdrawal. But I needed to get closure and start my emotional healing. I applied through the Toronto Police Headquarters to expunge my records, including fingerprints and photos, from their database.

Within six months, I received a letter from the Royal Canadian Mountain Police (RCMP) that they had deleted all the records. I was no longer in horror, reliving the nightmare I'd suffered.

After the temporary assignment ended, I got another at Kandoville Senior Public School. The distance to the school took almost two hours by bus, closer to the university where I studied. Although I spent a long time traveling on the subway, I found comfort in knowing the administrators valued me. I enjoyed going to work.

Mishika, the white vice-principal, had written a splendid reference letter before her retirement. *"Nadine has excellent interpersonal and problem-solving skills. She is calm, confident, professional, highly regarded, and respected by staff. It has been a pleasure working with Nadine."*

My self-esteem ballooned with these words of affirmation.

Nez was the principal. She was a stalwart and patient with impeccable manners, a Black woman who stood for equality. Her staff was multicultural, and many supported her. Lucie, her white vice-principal, often crafted false assertions. "Nez hired you because you go to the same church," she told me.

But Nez and I had never met before until I began the interim position at the school. Lucie constantly attempted to undermine me; she criticized my work ethic and was friendlier to the other two white office staff.

Without speaking to Lucie, Nez understood my dilemma. "Have a seat, Nadine. How is it going?"

As I sat down, water flooded my eyes.

"Wipe those tears, now. They're a sign of weakness. Don't let them see you crying. You're a strong woman. This job isn't easy. Lucie also humiliated me in meetings and made false accusations, but I stayed true to myself. Start seeking a permanent position because this is only temporary. My door is always open whenever you need to talk."

I smeared my face and took several deep breaths.

"That's right. Get out there with your head high."

Nez and Mishika inspired me and built my self-worth, so I felt ready to take on the world. I submitted my resume to a job posting for an Office Administrator position at Murchket Way Public School. The vice-principal interviewed me and recommended me for permanent employment.

I found myself a Black woman managing a school office within a white woman's territory where influences and acquaintances sometimes speak louder than integrity and experience. I had the title but no power to discuss direct or indirect issues affecting my work setting.

The photocopier and fax machine were across from my desk, so endless disruptions and deafening noises were in my ears. Students threw objects across the office. The white secretary's truancy, injunctions, and perpetual complaints became overwhelming. I spent my days wishing that the hours would pass quickly.

Ron, the disgruntled principal, moved the photocopier upstairs in the lounge but said he wasn't happy about it. "I can't see the staff because they're no longer coming to the office."

But I was finally at peace. The noise ceased, and no longer was I forced to inhale toxic fumes.

In the meantime, I planned for my highest achievement. I walked across the stage, and the Chancellor awarded me a Bachelor of Business Administration at June 2002 commencement. Mama commemorated the moment to honor the milestone in my life. Friends and family lavished me with pink and red roses, white and lilac flowers, and gifts expressing their love.

My degree was hard won. Looking back at the beginning, I got that degree, although the challenges were vast, both terrible and triumphant. Mama sat across the dining table and kept me company while

I was pulling in those late-night studies for exams. She was a proud mother; her last child had finished strong.

The Board relocated Ron, and his successor was Ritchie. He was a tall white man and used his power to advance his agenda. His frequent absences from the building were a red flag, but no one dared to query his whereabouts.

One afternoon, he approached me while I was alone in the office.

"Hey, Nadine. Deposit this." His gaze was stern and steady.

"What's that for?"

Ritchie gave me a cheque. "Open an account."

"This is a hefty amount of money. Is it for the school?"

"No."

"But we already have three bank accounts."

He knitted his eyebrow. "You're not going to do what I'm asking?"

"I'm uncomfortable opening another one."

He took back the cheque and hurried into the hallway.

I didn't know where or how he got the funds, but I refused to participate in any possible illegal activity. People from other ethnicities often perceived Blacks as dishonest. The notion of a Black woman involved in embezzlement was more believable than a white man. Therefore, I protected myself from this false narrative.

Ritchie was frustrated and angry. After that, he misled staff and the vice-principal into believing I was a problematic employee. His constant monitoring was infuriating, and it became impossible to work there. I knew my only way out was to apply for job postings. All I wanted was a stable job and to thrive. I did everything within my control to fly under the radar and performed an excellent job.

I had many successful interviews but no offers. In a conversation with one of my references, I learned Ritchie had made slanderous comments, blocking me from being hired. It was unfair, but I couldn't quit until I found another job.

The phone rang while moving toward the fax machine, and I rushed back to answer. "Good morning, Murchket Way Public School." It was late morning, and I was alone in the office.

"Hi, is this Nadine?"

"Speaking."

"Hello, I'm your union representative. I just received a call from your principal. He arranged a meeting for next Wednesday for you and wanted us there. Can you tell me what it's about?" Her voice was pleasant and supportive.

"He blamed me for not getting along with other staff. I tried leaving, but he gave me a bad evaluation. I'm weary and worried."

"You're entitled to your sick days if you're feeling stressed. Don't worry, Nadine. We'll be there."

"Okay. Thanks."

"Take care of yourself," she said.

Ritchie's plot to stop me from a job opportunity and possible discipline was frightening. I gawped at the blank computer screen and remembered my past. I was terrified, resurrecting the triggers and trauma of silencing and mistreatment. *It's the same act but a different place and time. If I could speak the truth, they wouldn't believe me anyway.* I felt I was caught in a nightmarish loop.

The recess bell rang, and I peeked through the office window. Children were giggling and playing tag outside. I smiled and wished I were a kid again. I loved working with them, and they kept me coming back.

At the meeting, Ritchie insisted, "Staff is afraid to talk to Nadine."

"Why don't you give her an outstanding reference since you're unhappy with her performance?" said the union rep. "Let her go."

He cleared his throat with a twisted smile and without saying a word.

After a brief pause, the rep said, "Please let her leave." We went our separate ways.

A few days later, I accepted a job offer from Grovebliss Senior Public School.

Chapter 4
Turning Point

The distance from home to work now took less than twenty minutes, so I was no longer riding the crammed, foul train and was instead catching up on well-deserved sleep. Grovebliss catered to grade seven and eight students with varying needs. Enna, the white principal, welcomed and introduced me to the teaching, custodial, and support staff. Her stylish cinnamon-colored blouse caught my eye. I was in my utopia once more. She embraced my communication and organizational skills and was eager to have me at her school.

Christmas and end-of-year parties highlighted the festivities and allowed staff to unwind. Enna planned the Spring party at her home. Each person chose a song from the hip-hop playlist. *"It wasn't me"* by Shaggy was one of the most popular lyrics of the evening. Some people danced while others laughed, listening to their favorite pop music. I grabbed chips and finger food. Everyone had a blast mingling.

June is always predictable and hectic in school. There's graduation as grade eight transitions to high school, and there are also class excursions. I was busy when Enna called me into her office and said, "I'm leaving for another school in September. I want you to know before anyone else."

I nodded—my hands damp with sweat. I opened the door, bolted outside, leaned against the metal fence, and sobbed, afraid of what would come next. "Why the change, after two perfect years, God? Please help me."

When I had recovered enough to talk about it, I went back to her office. "Enna, I'm sad you're leaving."

She smiled. "I'm not far away. You can call or visit me any time, Nadine."

"That's awesome." I felt reassured.

I had total freedom and leisure in July and August. I linked up with friends to movies and backyard barbecues. A church trip to Canada's Wonderland was one of the high points. The roller coaster and thrilling rides soaring seventy-five feet in the air were scary and not to my liking. Yet, I was impressed with the live performances, attractions, and the picnic we laid on the grass.

The sight of lush green valleys and ethereal beauty on the road trip to the Stratford Festival was mythical and consisted of theatrical productions of contemporary adaptations and musicals of Shakespeare plays. Magnificent! One of my favorites was *Romeo and Juliet*. Their overpowering force of emotions and love for each other defied society.

On my drive home, I thought, *This is true love.*

Despite the horrible challenges of the past year, my best moment was adopting my son, Jay. He was three years old, chirpy, and infused with energy. Between relaxing on the deck and shopping at the mall, sometimes we strode about the neighborhood or had strawberry ice cream cones at the corner store.

As summer ended, I prepared to return to work and organized my closet with the new clothing I had purchased. I matched my outfit with a pair of bangles and block-heel shoes. I had my hair shampooed and styled. My medium-layered haircut and dark brown highlights dazzled in the sun.

Some people said, "You're stunning, Nadine," when I walked into the staff room. I felt rejuvenated and was ready for the new year.

Chapter 5

Pressured But Not Crushed

Lise Nandez, the new principal, wore a rounded chin-length bob with bangs and always talked over others during a conversation. Daisy, the nosy educational assistant, constantly snooped and interfered in people's affairs. They were from the Philippines and joined forces together to create chaos.

A few days later, Daisy crossed her arms. "Where are you going?"

"Why do you want to know?"

She stood in my way, blocking me from going up the stairs, continuing with her barrage of questioning.

"Please move out my way," I said.

She stepped aside.

When I returned, I saw her coming through Lise's door with a tight-lipped smile.

Is she gossiping?

A Black student sat on the dark blue chair, staring at the art on the wall. The teacher sent him to the office because he snickered during his computer class. His eyes sparkled as he chatted with me about a soccer game he'd watched the weekend before.

Lise was suddenly outraged. "Don't talk to the students when they come here, Nadine."

"No problem."

But there was a problem. Lise stopped me from speaking to students and snapped the only lifeline from some troubled kids.

Whenever I left my desk, Lise questioned my whereabouts made me quite uncomfortable. The memory of how things could go wrong in an instant frightened me.

One day, I called the union office and expressed my concerns. It had been more than two years since I sought advice. I had a different rep because I was working in another region. She had been an office administrator for over fifteen years and was familiar with the school dynamics. Her words were charged with authority but cheerful.

"How about we arrange a meeting with you and the principal?"

"Are you attending?

"Yes."

Everything became more apparent when we met. Lise moved her chair closer to me and threw accusations my way. "You're hiding information from me and avoiding my questions."

"I don't know how Enna allocated the budget."

"Didn't you and Enna work together, and she shared everything with you?"

"You're right, we had a cohesive relationship, but

she never discussed the budget with me." The principal is expected to allot money to classrooms, resources, and textbooks based on the teacher's requests. Not all principals involve their office administrator in decision-making because it's their prerogative. In keeping with this practice, I refrained from being intrusive and followed only directives.

"Oh," she hesitated.

Her demeanor changed a bit after the clarification. She tried collaborating, sought my opinion, and invited me to leadership meetings. Although we made progress, several teachers' complaints about her disrespect resulted in a superintendent swapping principals between schools.

Based on my years of experience, my skepticism about new administrators was much higher than others. I had the instinct to exercise discretion. Everybody had a backstory, but one never knew what it was until it was exposed. Armelia Benduse, an Italian principal, and Lise's successor, displayed a pleasant persona the first time we met. Her persistence to snatch me from my shell (a protective shield to avoid undesirable workplace emotional abuse and pain) was admirable but mentally draining.

"Nadine, you don't say much. Why?"

"No reason. I want to focus on doing my job."

"Don't you share your thoughts and feelings?"

"What do you want from me?"

"I care about you, Nadine."

"Well, I don't trust anyone."

"How can you live like that?" Her eyes filled with tears.

These words resounded and plagued me for days. *My life is fraught with fears and fatigue.*

The next day, I was sitting at my computer, completing a petty cash reimbursement, when Armelia burst into laughter as she rambled. "Hello, Nadine. Didn't get much sleep last night?"

"No. I guess you've already noticed."

I shook my head and sighed. The thought of trusting Armelia was devastating, but we made a pact to trust each other. Over time, I became courageous, and my hidden talents and beauty shimmered.

As I found contentment in coming to work and letting go of my fears, the inevitable happened. In Armelia's narrowed office, I sat at the edge of my chair. I could sense the indifference coming from her. "Nadine, the staff is complaining you're not approachable, and they're afraid of you."

"Armelia, I'm confused. Can't you see what they're doing?"

"I don't understand."

"They want me out because I'm Black." In a split second, I remembered Jezebella, Shier, and Nancita's collaboration resulted in severe discipline. Now, I was facing a similar difficulty. Over the years, white folks targeted, silenced, scrutinized, isolated, and branded me as "creating a negative work environment" or not getting along with people. These practices stemmed from slavery and colonialism.

It was effortless for other races to blame me for their harassment, belittlement, condescension, hostility, and alienation. Making these claims was a diversion from their anti-Black racism. With this practice, it was easier to deny the existence of racism and defend the status quo. The institutional system in Canada functioned on these ideologies, designed to preserve white power and privileges.

"But . . . so many?"

"Who are they?" I was shocked.

"No, I can't tell you." She left without saying one extra word. From my past, I knew the words "many, everyone, or everybody" meant one person or a supervisor.

Moving back to my desk, I spotted Mitsy and Rosecca eyeing me. Mitsy, a white secretary, detested having a Black person in charge, which was indicative of prejudice. Rosecca, a white vice-principal, called herself a "white belly fish." She used this term to reinforce her whiteness, maybe even without knowing it was a racist statement.

Because of Armelia's inability to gain an unbiased perspective, she was trapped between their jealousy and conspiracy.

I became aloof, alone in a dark room during breaks and lunches. In those moments, I wept like a small child. My voice was diminished to complete silence, and the trust ended.

Carlos, a Black guidance teacher, got caught in the crossfire. He didn't recognize the secretary and administrators were using him as their collaborator in their attack against me. They approved whatever he requested, and he got away with not complying with policies and procedures.

One afternoon in June, Carlos stood at the office door. "Nadine, I'm leaving the students in the meeting room to arrange the grade eight's records."

"Are you leaving them unsupervised?"

"Yes."

"Alone with the confidential records?"

He screamed, his sudden outburst terrifying me. "What do you want me to do? It's your job." My role was to organize the records by the school. Carlos assisted in the process.

A man screaming at me was my breaking point. I cursed, and he stopped shouting. I hastened into the filing room, shut the door, and squatted on the floor, bewildered. My mind flashed to a dream I had a few months ago.

I was at an airport, ready to board a flight. A woman dressed in black and white instructed me to a separate entrance leading inside an empty room. There was no visible exit. After going around in circles, trying to escape, a door opened to an airplane.

I noticed strange faces on the jet, laughing and gawking at me. The flight was tumultuous; I held tight to my seat until the plane landed on an island surrounded by an ocean. I removed my shoes and walked in the water along the shore alone, not knowing where I was going. I felt rejected, lost, and without any lifelines.

Footsteps sounded in the office; I stood on my feet and braced my back against the wall until they faded before I hustled outside.

It had been a taxing week. My grandmother had died, and my dad was battling lung cancer and had one month to live. Being overwhelmed with stress, my lower body spasmed, and I lost movement for a few minutes.

Days later, Armelia slapped me with a disciplinary letter for swearing at Carlos. If I were white, this would never have transpired. Racism would not have been a factor, and I wouldn't have been in a situation where I had no one on my side. Moreover, white folks swore at each other daily, which management regarded as an acceptable norm. I knew I was in a bad situation, and it wouldn't be easy to escape without tearing down everything I had built.

Chapter 6
Father Passing

Astley, my father, was tall, had brown eyes, and a sense of humor. He was known for his generosity and patience. Although he had limited resources, his passion for helping the homeless made him famous in his community. In his early years as a minister, he stood by a mother with the strong belief that her child would recover from a severe illness. And she did.

Over the years, we built a special father-daughter relationship and communicated frequently while we lived in separate countries. Whenever I visited Jamaica, he would provide my favourite fruits, including sweet sugar cane and mangoes.

That Tuesday evening in May 2009, as I was in my bedroom packing the suitcase to leave for my grandmother's funeral in Jamaica, I phoned my sister, Shurry, who also lived in Jamaica, to inform her of my visit and intention to see my father on Friday.

Shurry was elated to hear the good news and agreed to accompany me.

A few minutes later, the phone rang as I continued to pack. I glanced at the call display and realized it was Shurry.

"Hi, Shurry. Is everything okay?" I asked.

"Not really." She answered.

"What are you saying?"

"Dad is diagnosed with cancer."

"Oh, no! When did you learn about this?"

"Recently."

"Thanks for the information. I'll see you on Friday."

After I hung up the phone, I paced the room, reminiscing about the special moments we shared. I remember at 12 years old, my dad sang to me, "When I was just a little girl, I asked my mother, what will I be? Will I be pretty? Will I be rich? Here's what she said to me. Que sera, sera, whatever will be, will be; the future's not ours to see. Que sera, sera, what will be, will be." The tears filled my eyes as I thought about him, and the most beautiful song ever sung to me by my father.

On Thursday afternoon, I arrived in Jamaica. I had mixed emotions about the death of my grandmother and my father's illness.

The following day, I visited my dad and brought him gifts. He smiled at me, although he was in excruciating pain. I walked over to him, hugged him, and said, "l love you, Daddy." And he nodded his head.

After spending hours with him, I left thinking I might not see him alive again.

On June 30, 2009, one week into summer vacation, my dad succumbed to his illness. He had been fighting lung cancer for several months. I had already planned a seven-night Caribbean cruise to celebrate my forty-second birthday with Mama and Jay, and I desperately needed some time away from all the stress, so I was looking forward to it.

I was sailing for the first time, and the beautiful sun setting over the water was breathtaking. We stopped on the exotic islands. I lounged on the beach while the ship docked at Half Moon Cay, Bahamas. My mind drifted away from the year's traumatic events as I listened to the gushing sound of the waves and melodic music. I stared upward into the sky, thinking of sheer freedom.

I wore a light beige hat and a brown, yellow, and black patterned swimsuit. Mama's white t-shirt and blue jeans skirt fit her perfectly. Jay's grey cap and red swim shorts made him stand out in the crowd. We were posing in our sunglasses, leaning against the blue and white Carnival Liberty signage. And I imagined myself a model in Vogue or Elle magazines.

Grand Turk stretched 7 miles (11 km) long and 1.5 miles (2.41 km) wide. We explored the island within four hours, stunned at seeing the free-range giant Iguana lizards walking on the ground. My heart beat fast as I tiptoed sideways.

San Juan, Puerto Rico, had world-class dining and shopping. I connected with Calvin, using the free WIFI at a McDonald's restaurant. As I trudged around, I enjoyed the sound of jazz music and the sight of the colorful century-old buildings. It was surreal living like a celebrity.

After the ship docked in St. Maarten, we strolled down the beach. It was late afternoon as I relaxed on the white sandy shore. A hot breeze blew against me. Jay's laughter rang in the air as the wave dashed against his sandcastles. I smiled, feeling free.

On a formal night, Mama dressed in a satin maroon dress, while Jay looked handsome in his grey suit and tie, and I had on an off-white two-piece outfit. The lights glowed. *Wow! So much more than I expected!* My mind drifted to a fairytale story I'd read as a young girl. I remember thinking I was the lovely Black princess at my enchanted royal ball this time.

My worries disappeared. I felt immersed in relaxation and distracted by the fun until the day before going home. As I stood in line, waiting for breakfast, I got dizzy and almost fainted. Two strangers held me before I collapsed to the floor. Distraction only goes so far.

I didn't get to say goodbye, and he's gone, I thought. *I must face my father's death.*

I was grateful to have had the chance to see my dad six weeks before his death when I attended my grandmother's funeral. While he was frail, we had time to talk, hug, and told him how much I loved him.

The month of August was overwhelming both with grieving the loss of my father and the impending discipline. The stress was overwhelming, so I phoned the union office and spoke with Mirielle.

"I'm sorry to hear about your loss. What support did you receive from your principal?"

"None."

"Let me make a few calls and get back to you,

Nadine."

The following day Mirielle rang me. I leaned against the staircase handrail with the cordless phone at my ear. The sun shifted from the east to the west side of my house. It was still sweltering outside but excellent inside because of the air conditioner.

"Hi, Nadine. How are you feeling today?"

"Anxious."

"I informed Jerraine about the disciplinary letter and your loss. She agreed to an external mediator as an alternative to discipline. I also spoke with Carlos' union, but he didn't file any complaint against you. We'll take care of everything for you."

"Thank you very much."

Jerraine, the white Superintendent of Education, was empathetic and caring. She was Armelia's boss and had the disciplinary letter rescinded. She had become involved after the union filed a grievance against Armelia. Instead of handling the matter herself, she appointed a mediator.

I returned to work at the end of August 2009 for a few days, but Jerraine kept me at home during the mediation process.

In those two months of waiting, I plunged into a deep depression. I closed my bedroom blinds and blocked the light from coming inside. I had an aching brain and no energy or appetite.

What was before me, I could not see as anything but a passage through a long dark tunnel.

Finally, I got my job back. I took one anti-anxiety

pill the night before going back to work in November. The mediator escorted me inside to make the transition easier. Never in my life had I felt so uneasy, looking at a photo of a train glued to the wall, white faces looking through the window. My entire office area had been whitewashed.

Mitsy dumped my mug and personalized notepads in the trash. She arranged the office, erasing everything I did and making it her own. She was acting in my position and receiving extra pay in my absence. It stopped after I returned, so she wasn't happy to see me.

She handed over the files without any comments.

"Thank you," I said.

She didn't reply.

The next afternoon, Armelia invited me to a meeting. The space was small, a rectangular table with six chairs. Mitsy and Armelia were sitting across from me, and Rosecca was to my right. Armelia threw a sheet of paper with my job description on the table. "Mitsy doesn't want you to assign her work. Let her decide what she wants to do since she has been doing your job for three months."

I was rather shocked at her sudden outburst; I could only deflect. "Armelia, can someone from the union and employee services resolve who does what?"

"No."

Seven days later, I received a written notice from the Board's Human Rights investigator. Mitsy filed a workplace harassment complaint. In her statement, she said, "After the meeting, I left very emotionally . . . I pulled over on the side of the road as I ended up in a panic attack. Nadine told me, I and the vice-principal go running to Mommy whenever we have a problem. She had no eye contact or a friendly manner. She was belittling, isolated me, aggressive, rude, and a difficult person."

Whites warped these claims to uphold systematic racism, superiority, and fragility. Any accusation of this kind would lead to demotion, progressive discipline, or have a negative effect on future promotions.

During the investigation, I often worked in the filing room, sitting at a student's desk to avoid more lies, humiliation, and hostility. Rosecca stood at the entrance watching and lowered her eyebrows.

Mitsy was insecure and threatened that a Black woman was more educated than her. She eavesdropped on a telephone conversation I had with a past colleague who wanted to know if I had completed my courses.

Armelia stepped from her office. "Nadine, Mitsy told me you're talking about your education."

"But I was answering a question on the phone."

"I want you to stop," Armelia demanded.

Meanwhile, the year-end party was fast approaching, but I had no interest in a work-related social gathering. Mitsy observed that my name was missing from the attendee list. She threw it on my desk, scoffed, "You're not a team player," and walked away.

Not one person consoled me. I had no ally except

the truth, but nobody believed me.

Alfanso, an occasional teacher, approached me while I was sitting in the staffroom alone in a daze. "Nadine, how are you?"

"Frazzled. I'm trying not to take another anti-anxiety pill. I don't want to become addicted."

"Well, don't take anymore. Close your eyes. Imagine you're watching a movie, and you're the star. What do you see?"

"A sad person."

"What kind words do you want to say to her?"

"You're beautiful."

"How is she now?"

"Smiling and happy."

After the exercise, I became empowered. "Thank you for helping me."

"No. You did everything yourself."

I didn't comprehend what occurred but left with a new mindset.

The verdict came in from the Human Rights department in February 2010, "Nadine White has violated the Board's Workplace Harassment Policy . . ."

Mitsy accomplished her plan to remove me, ruin my character, and position herself for my job. Her sister-in-law and Rosecca were the primary witnesses and backed her story. They successfully misconstrued and distorted my words to maintain their white privilege.

Chapter 7
Obstacles Into Opportunities

The emotional pain gripped my inner mind as I exited the building. On the verge of a mental breakdown, my counselor encouraged me. "Take walks every day, even when you don't want to. Listen to your favorite songs and repeat scripture verses that inspire you."

In desperation, I asked, "Why are they getting away with their actions?"

"They're not. Their time will come."

Everything halted during a Sunday morning church service. No sermon. My pastor brought attention to my situation. Her spoken affirmations amazed me because she had zero knowledge of my misery until the Holy Spirit revealed it to her. As I stood speechless before the congregation, everyone strode in a single file and embraced me.

Each song and uplifting words touched my heart. Tears flowed down my face. "God, you did this for me?"

I kept quiet as I drove home with Mama and Jay that early afternoon, mesmerized by God's presence. With the sun fading, I gazed at the cloudy sky. The gentle breeze lifted the end of my thin red, blue, and brown scarf.

Mama opened the door and went into the kitchen. I kicked off my black suede leather tall-top boots and hung up my coat in the closet. I hurried upstairs to my room, picked up my notebook, and began to write.

Dear Diary, today, March 21, 2010, has been my best day. The Lord exceptionally visited me. Awesome! Thank you, Holy Spirit, for your divine intercession. You reminded me that you're with me. You heard my cry and prayers. You love me so much you gave me your full attention today. I appreciate you, and you're my everything.

One month later, I received a disciplinary letter from the Superintendent of Education.

Dear Nadine White,

This letter confirms the details of a disciplinary meeting held on March 11, 2010, at 1:00 p.m., to discuss the results of the Workplace Harassment investigation related to a complaint originating from Grovebliss.

Based on the Human Rights Office investigation, we have concluded that your actions contributed to a poisonous atmosphere in your school. You told the complainant not to bother the principal, and all staff has the right to speak to the principal. You may not block staff lines of communication.

During a meeting with the principal, vice-principal, and complainant, you repeatedly referred to the complainant in the third person and did not acknowledge her presence. You referred to her as "the clerical," which was inappropriate. Inclusive language is essential for working together and building teams.

You used the expression "running to mommy" or implied something similar when the complainant or others went to the principal with concerns. The use of demeaning language and intimidation is unacceptable.

In addition, you are required to participate in Anger Management and Team Building training. I must caution you that any further misconduct will result in more serious disciplinary action." I lost my job at this location.

Their insults and belittlement infuriated me.

As a part of the castigation, the Board placed me in an acting Office Administrator position at another school in March 2010. Jorge, a Greek principal, was sympathetic and respectful, yet I stayed professional and prudent.

Each day, I gained inner strength and hope. My energy level soared. I laughed again, vacuumed, and dusted the furniture at home.

In the final session in therapy on June 6, 2010, my counselor was pleased with my progress. My groggy mind struggled to make sense of all this. I never realized depression made me gloomy. As a literal fact, I could no longer fathom where I had been until I was mentally healed—transitioned from darkness to light.

"Was I in a dark place?" I asked the counselor, baffled by the phenomenon.

"Your faith in God and willpower brought you through." She answered carefully.

"Please help me understand . . . ?"

"Yes."

"How many people have been there and recovered?"

"Not many."

Beyond the hopelessness, sadness, loss of appetite, and lack of interest in social activities, I never contemplated suicide, but kept a journal of my feelings and thoughts. I opened my windows, although I forbade the intrusion of light inside. Often, I walked when I had no passion. I danced to the music while watching the *Ellen DeGeneres Show*.

I feasted on sitcom comedy: *Everybody Loves Raymond, Golden Girls, Friends,* and *The Fresh Prince of Bel-Air*.

Books such as *The Prayer of Jabez, Never Give Up, The Battlefield of the Mind,* and *Joy for a Woman's Soul* were inspirational and encouraging. Some of the most important messages came from *Joel Osteen, Joyce Myers,* and *T.D. Jakes*.

Dear Diary, I looked back, went through a wilderness, and got lost; I did not realize how dark it was until I saw the light at the end. The months were dismal, and I lost my mind, but God was with me. The hugs, smiles, and encouragement helped me. The cycle has broken, and there are more incredible blessings for me in the future. I'll go forward with self-confidence, open to and embrace life more meaningfully. I choose to be positive because I know God ordered my steps.

The acting position ended, and the staffing administrator placed me in a permanent position at M.J. Stonesworth. Principal Nelly, a Black woman, interrogated me for two hours, which was intimidating and unnecessary.

"Please let me understand the reasons you're doing this?" I said.

"They sent you here without having a chance to interview."

"Okay . . ."

My eyes welled with tears as I stepped outside. In the distance, I could hear birds twittering. *Do I want to work here? What to do in this predicament? Some administrators don't like the Board placing staff in their schools without their final say. I'm misplaced. If I could wave a magic wand, I wouldn't be here either. I must prove myself, and I'm not too fond of that.*

Jorge gave me a gift card. "Nadine, working with you over the past 3 1/2 months was wonderful. I wish you all the best at your new school and remember to stay positive! Don't forget to call me if you need directions. Take care of yourself and your family."

"Thank you, Jorge, for these kind words."

On July 10, 2010, Mama, Jay, and I vacationed at Varadero, Cuba, lodged for a week at the Iberostar five-star, all-inclusive hotel. I was bewitched by the theatrical performances and intoxicated with the rhythms of salsa dancing.

We toured Havana, a treasure of historic colonial reserves; the buildings were European style and resembled cars from the 1950s. It was eye-catching. Carriages with horses and coachmen strolled through the street, going to varying destinations, replicas of medieval times.

When I asked one of the servers for a non-alcoholic drink, she said, "Would you like Sex on the beach?"

"What's that?" I asked, blushing.

"Mostly fruit juices."

"I'll try it. Add only a dash of vodka."

She nodded and left with a grin.

Within minutes, she returned with a chilled cocktail in a highball glass garnished with an orange slice. It was delicious—a change from drinking soda pop.

Friday was my birthday. Following breakfast, I strolled along the beach with absolute gratitude and reflected on God's inventions. The clear sky, warm sunrise, and steady waves added to the sense of calm.

Father, thank you for this beautiful day! Your creation, incredible ocean, gentle breeze, and life. Celebrating my birthday with someone exceptional would be neat, but I'm grateful my family is with me.

In the bedroom, a bottle of wine was on the ring-shaped table, wrapped in a red ribbon—a spectacular white towel origami of an elephant with rose petals on my bed. I cackled with glee, seeing a lovely gesture.

The trip was over, and I was back in Canada, but the memory had been tattooed forever on my brain.

Dear diary, Nor finished painting the house. What a relief! Six long weeks for the handyman to paint *the downstairs and upstairs. No kitchen, bedrooms, or bathrooms for $4000.*

Many things I accomplished this summer: organized my closet, donated clothing to the Diabetic Foundation, washed the garage, cleaned windows, and bought new outfits. I didn't get to hang up the chandelier or take my winter jackets to the dry cleaner. But that's okay, right?

I'm finally at my happy place, learning to love myself and accept the things I can't change. I don't want to relive those terrible and unpleasant moments. I've moved on and am trying to have positive influences. I believe that there are more incredible things for me to experience. God's favor and mercy keep showing in my life.

Chapter 8
Staying Afloat

Engaging our Black students to volunteer in the office permitted them to gain real-world experiences and boost their confidence. Most white administrators and staff failed to acknowledge the stereotypes and implicit biases towards Black kids that demoralized their self-esteem. Given a safe space for them to shine, they approached their future with positivism and a reason to succeed.

A parent was impressed with the positive change in her child's demeanor since she'd started volunteering. Her absenteeism decreased. She dressed up on the day she helped in the office. The mother requested, "If the school has a problem with my child, let her speak with Nadine."

But the white vice-principal recoiled. "You're playing good cop against the bad." She leaned against her office door jam, giving me a long flat stare until she moved away. She described herself as a "bad cop" because of her inability to connect with the Black students. Besides her frustration in that arena, the spotlight had shifted to me. Her inflated ego drove her to blurt out those words.

Dear Diary, today is May 23, 2011.

I've been working on my insecurities. I learned to accept myself and am trying to build positive relationships. There were times I felt I was drowning and needed rescuing. One way to get past the hurt and pain is forgiveness.

God, forgive every individual for hurting me. I will release them to you. I no longer wish my past to hold me hostage. I'm surrendering everything to you, things I have no control over. I'm also practicing letting go of situations and individuals that created or triggered anxiety and fear. I'm not where I would like to be, but it's a work in progress to be emotionally stable and grounded. You're awesome!

May gave way to June, and the days had been hectic with Nelly's retirement and planning for the upcoming September. I skimmed through an email from Superintendent Jerraine. She wanted me to phone her. *For what? I didn't hear from her since I left Grovebliss. It's been a year. Why now? What does she want?* I immediately spiraled into anxiety.

It took over an hour to muster up the courage to phone her.

"Hello."

"This is Nadine. You asked me to call you."

"Yes. How are you, Nadine?"

"I'm doing well."

"That's good." She paused a second longer, gathering her thoughts.

"There's an opportunity for you to attend professional development (PD) in Durham on June 3rd."

"Why? It's been a long time, Jerraine." My heart

hammered in my chest, thinking it might be another setup for me to fail and one more checked box on their list. *They always chose to send me for mentoring with a white person less educated than me or an anger management course. What's this professional development? No specifics of what to expect. To learn to get along with white folks. Am I an angry Black woman who needs self-control and to act appropriately?*

"Yes, I know. I was giving you time. Nadine, I would like you to go."

"Okay, I will."

"I'll send you the information and arrange coverage with Nelly."

I was reluctant, but I considered it a positive rather than a negative.

The day I arrived at the convention center, I met with the mediator. His sessions involved, *Understanding & Maintaining Interpersonal Boundaries and Violence & Harassment in the Workplace.* We were sitting at the table just before the conference began, and he said, "Jerraine is a tough one. It took me some time to convince her to send you to the PD."

I smiled. So, the mediator was the one who needed me here. I didn't know his motive and didn't care to ask.

Dan Carter was white and tall with sleepy eyes. He was the keynote speaker, not a household name such as Kenneth Copeland, Dr. David Jeremiah, or Charles Stanley, but he had an inspiring story that caught my attention.

He encountered many hurdles: losing his birth mother when he was months old, the death of his eldest brother, being raped as a young boy, drug addiction, depression, lack of self-confidence, living under bridges, and wandering around the cold streets at night.

As I listened, his story triggered my memory. His hardships got me thinking of my struggles and upheavals. I found my thoughts drifting to the man I once loved. I dated Willie for five years. Tall, dark, and witty. When he first saw me, his pupils dilated. At first, I glanced at him while he glided through the hallway. I couldn't stop thinking of him.

On our first date, we decided to have tea at the Just Dessert restaurant in the suburbs. He leaned against my shoulder and laughed at my silly jokes. Something about his humor made me content. I wondered what life would be like if we were still together. *I'm alone going through racial discrimination. I wish he were here holding my hands, telling me everything would be fine. I'm here for you.*

I drew a slow deep breath. Dan found his way and used his triumph to impact lives. *I could be writing my story one day.* His message of hope empowered me to take the next step on my journey. To find my purpose in bad times and open my heart again.

Jerraine wandered in late at Nelly's retirement party. She stood at the entrance, scanning the crowd until she saw me. We strode towards the dessert table and quickly hugged. "Delightful seeing you again, Nadine."

"Me too."

"Let's plan to have tea soon."

"Sure. I would like that."

On my way home, I was overjoyed. *Small steps were a victory,* and s*omeone believed in me. Anything can happen with the right mindset.*

Holidays to the Caribbean Islands were my haven during the summer. It was a time to frolic on the white sandy beach, bopping to reggae music and sampling an assortment of authentic cuisine under the stars, or gazing at the orange hue sunset in Negril, Jamaica. But this summer was more of a staycation because I was saving for a new car. Instead, I went on day trips to Ontario Place, the Exhibition, and connections.

Jerraine and I had an early afternoon brunch at Milestone on July 6, 2011. The incredible serenity and atmosphere on the outdoor patio had taken possession of my soul. We were graced with a warm breeze as people went in and out of the shopping mall. Others left the theatre, sipping from gigantic cups.

Jerraine said, "Look around and consider how beautiful it is. There are lovely and caring individuals in this world. We often surround ourselves with a few negative people until we forget the good ones."

I poured a cup of tea. "So true."

"When I was a young girl, my family and I immigrated to a foreign country before we came to Canada. English wasn't our first language. They called us names. The truth is, I could change my language." She hesitated, then resumed, "You can't change your skin color because this is who you are. I can't imagine how you must feel."

My head was spinning, and I was speechless. I processed every word she spoke, remembering her endorsing the mediation process. She kept me at home for two months. The day she phoned me, she asked me how I was doing. "I would like you to stay home longer, but the Board pressured me to send you back to work. You'll be placed at another school until the mediation wraps up." *Now, it makes sense.*

"I forgave them," I answered.

"How?"

"I learned forgiveness isn't for those who did me wrong. I can begin to heal from the pain and hurt by letting go. I'm not saying it's easy, but I practiced until it got better."

Jerraine bowed and shifted on her chair. She fixed her eyes on me, "Nadine, opportunities await you."

She handed me a card. "Don't open it until your birthday."

"Thank you for everything."

"You're welcome."

After we left, I jumped in my blue Pontiac Sunfire car with my windows down, going east at one hundred kilometers on the highway until I reached home.

Dear diary, This is another milestone, an afternoon that will forever resonate with me. I'm happy people cared for me, and my life is going in the right direction.

Father, I thank you for your favor and divine blessing. You've enlarged my territory and blessed me. I give you all the glory and honor. Amen.

I hopped out of bed after I prayed. "Lord, I welcome another year. I surrender everything to you. Today, July 16, I'm hopeful better days are ahead." Right away, I opened Jerraine's envelope. Inside was a pastel green colored card with printed pink, red, and white bouquets.

Dear Nadine,

Happy Birthday!

I wish you a wonderful summer, a birthday, and a new year filled with many fulfilled possibilities.

Kindly,

Jerraine K.

I placed it back on my dresser, brushed my teeth, and went downstairs to the kitchen. Mama sang to me. Jay arranged breakfast on the table. He huddled against me, giving me a bear hug.

Later in the afternoon, I joined my dear friend Alicia at the Town Centre. We watched the new film release, *Horrible Bosses,* a 2011 American comedy. Three friends, Nick (Jason Bateman), Dale (Charlie Day), and Kurt (Jason Sudeikis), were employees who conspired to kill their evil bosses. Besides being hilarious, I couldn't stop thinking of my experiences with awful administrators.

Long after I arrived home, I opened my gifts, chronicling my day's events: A pajama set, cards, hard cash, and birthday wishes via text messages and telephone calls, plus one vanilla cupcake with yellow icing and glitters on top. Earlier, I posed for several shots at Sears photo studio.

The photographer's collage was my perfect gift to capture a lifetime memory. I hung it on the wall in the family room above the entertainment unit. Peering at the photographs, I thought, *Gosh, I'm a gorgeous Black woman.*

Not only did I have a memorable summer, but I was also looking forward to an exciting new school year.

Chapter 9
What Happened Next?

Chaostina, a white principal who'd replaced Nelly, swung her arms back and forth while walking. Jane was white and had prolonged eye contact in conversations. She filled a vacant half-time secretary position. They'd worked together at a previous site and started at the same time at M.J. Stonesworth.

A teacher approached me in the staff room over lunch in September. "Did you hear what happened?"

"No. Why do you ask?"

"A student fell down the stairs."

"How?"

"I'm not sure."

"Perhaps they want my help."

I put my food back into my blue striped bag and rushed to help, but no one was in the office. The telephone lines rang nonstop, and I answered them. "Hello, M.J. Stonesworth."

"Is this Nadine?"

"Yes."

"Can I speak with Chaostina Tilet?"

"Hold, please."

"Ms. Tilet, there's a call on line 103."

She strolled to my desk. I handed her the phone.

While speaking, I overheard her saying, "I couldn't ask Nadine for help because she is on her lunch."

When she hung up, I asked, "Is there anything I can do for you?" Student safety took precedence over my lunch. If the student needed medical care, I would call an ambulance.

Chaostina's eyes hardened, and her face flushed. "No!" she shouted. She turned and stormed away.

Not a single word could describe the mayhem in the school. Chaostina alerted upper management and the entire Board that a student had fallen. Jane walked around, trying to figure out what to do.

Dear Diary,

A challenging time at work. Jane has been very cruel to me since September. She's overbearing and continuously harassing me. She held her hand and said, "Don't talk to me." Her eyes were wild, and she was acting like a crazy person.

After I reported her rude behavior to the principal, she lied and said parents and staff were having a problem with me. Chaostina Tilet can't be trusted. She took the office key from me and asked me to write my daily work and when I left to use the restroom. These are signs of unfair treatment, and it's discriminatory.

The best thing about this, I practiced surrendering everyone and everything to God. I'm releasing His wisdom, peace, joy, self-control, and strength to overcome these burdens. He's my protector.

Thank you, Lord. October 23, 2011.

Many times, Jane scorned and taunted me. One morning, she yelled, stomped out of the office, and slammed the door. Horrified, I spoke with Chaostina, and she responded, "Contact your union rep if you have a problem."

"But I believe you can resolve the issue."

She threw her hands in the air and shut her door.

Immediately, I rang the Superintendent's office and disclosed Jane's uncontrollable tantrum. "Did you talk to your principal?" The administrative liaison asked.

"Yes."

"What did she say?"

"Speak with your union rep. But I didn't. I thought she could easily deal with the situation. I'm not feeling safe."

"Okay, I'll make a note."

"Thank you."

The days that followed were dehumanizing and distressing. Chaostina had me log in when I left my desk to go to the toilet. Jane rummaged through my mailbox. I was infuriated, but I kept silent. I didn't want any backlash.

Next to my desk, an Indian teacher was checking his binder. He watched and listened to my telephone conversation. I was uncertain why he occupied the chair, but I was terrified to query. Days after, Jane mentioned I didn't help him when he asked for my assistance. But that wasn't true.

My survival depended on lunch prayers with two other Black staff members. But it was short-lived after Chaostina intervened, saying prayer wasn't appropriate on campus. We were afraid to converse in public. Sometimes I perched, secluded, under the stairs.

Late Thursday morning, November 1, 2011, when passing Jane's desk, I had a sudden suspicion; something terrible was about to happen. Her glaring eyes and grin convinced me.

I bolted from the office to the staffroom and rang Calvin. He was an Elementary teacher and taught grade 6.

"The secretary is filing harassment against me."

"Who told you?"

"No one. I don't know how to explain."

"Don't jump to any conclusions."

"You don't understand."

"Let's talk later."

My head was spinning, claustrophobic, as though the walls were closing in on me. *It can't be happening again.*

The next day, I filed harassment complaints to the Board's Human Rights office against Chaostina and Jane. I couriered the documents with Purolator. I didn't want to delay or stay mute this time, unlike what I'd done with Mitsy's allegation. Somebody needed to consider my story.

Wednesday, November 7, at 11:30 a.m., the Board

sent me home during the investigation. I wasn't permitted to contact anyone at work, and the Board denied me access to my email.

In my initial meeting, the investigator mentioned Jane filed harassment against me, but they had received my claim first. *I was right. It must have been the Holy Spirit who had spoken to me that morning.* She went through a series of questions, seeking clarifications.

In August, I began wearing braces, impeding my pronunciation when responding, so I spoke slowly for accuracy.

There was another force at play here, something I never denied. The unfavorable outcome of Mitsy's accusation had been fifteen months and two weeks prior. Before, it was a white man, and now, a white woman was investigating. I was scared by them blaming me again and considering this as a pattern of behavior. My voice broke, and the sob reinforced my pain. *The investigator has the power to destroy me.*

Though I filed the harassment first, she called me again to interrogate me. A whispering voice inside my head knew she had doubted me.

The union steward said, "Nadine, you told your truth. Let's wait for the result."

Dear Diary,

I can't believe the month of January is almost finished. Time goes fast. For this reason, I've decided to enjoy each day to the fullest. I was getting anxious, but I thanked God for waking me up. I have all my senses.

A new day to relish; not concerned with yesterday or tomorrow. Today is a gift from the creator. He's in control and working on my behalf, even when I don't see or feel it; This is what believing is. The Bible says faith is the substance of things, hope for the evidence of things not seen.

My confidence entered another level; the worry and fear disappeared, and this was a breakthrough.

Thank you, God, for taking care of me. You're awesome!

Friday, January 20, 2012

Chapter 10
A Spiritual Encounter

Dear Diary,

Today, Tuesday, January 24, 2012, I'm fasting and seeking God's guidance and directions. I cried out, Lord, please help me and reveal yourself. I'm empty and broken. I'm in this wilderness (a dry place) and don't know where to go. I'm crying out to you, Father, for answers, but it seems you're not here. Where are the people who supported me in the beginning? Right here and now, I don't understand and can't make sense of all this.

I'm on a journey and confident you're in everything. Why? Where is the destination? I'm looking for assurance God is leading the way. I need to follow and trust him because he knows all things.

My car broke down when I pulled out from the orthodontist parking lot. I phoned roadside assistance. While I waited, I hunched over the steering wheel, rubbing my swollen eyes. "My world is falling apart."

In less than an hour, the tow truck arrived, and the driver asked, "Where are you taking your car?"

"To the nearest dealer."

"The cost is twice the amount! "I'll take you to my mechanic. Not far from here."

He hooked up my car to the back of his truck

and drove to the garage. Checking the vehicle, the mechanic identified that I needed a new battery, spark plugs, and other repairs. He only replaced the critical parts, and I paid less than I would at the dealer.

Miracles happen through people.

On Sunday morning, February 5, 2012, my phone rang.

"Hello, Calvin."

"Are you going to church today?

"No."

"Why?"

"I don't want to."

"Talk to you later."

After I hung up, I lay in bed with my eyes closed. In a spiritual encounter, God told me, "It's not about work. I'm still working on you." I saw a medium-sized red clay vase fall to the ground and shatter. I didn't see anyone, but I heard a gentle voice say, "This represents the brokenness of your life, struggles, and broken relationships. Each crack is your pain; the scars are your fears and insecurity. I want to heal you. For this reason, I separated you from the world."

He put the vase back together. "You'll return to work when I heal you."

I felt the tears oozing down my face onto the pillow. "Lord, forgive me for my lack of knowledge and understanding."

When I was in God's presence, nothing in the world mattered. I was safe and complete. His love and grace became alive. I was overwhelmed with his mercies for the first time because I saw him for who he was.

My eyes snapped open. I rolled off the bed and grabbed the Bible from the nightstand. The chocolate drapes and neutral color blinds shut. Beyond the pale blue shade bathroom window, the sky filled with the glowing sunrise. I flicked the light switch in the bedroom, lying on my stomach and turning the pages. "Agree with your adversary quickly, while you are in their way; before your adversary brings you to the judge, and he delivers you to the officer and casts you into prison" (Matt. 5:25).

How can I agree with them? It isn't sincere, but God is wise.

"Be not afraid or dismayed of this great multitude; for the battle is not yours, but God's . . ." (2 Chr. 20:15).

The voice continued, "I will put people on your path to help you."

I was in awe of God's supernatural intervention and sovereignty. Any doubt I had of God's written words in the bible was no longer in my mind from that day. *Nothing is like the voice of God. That joy supersedes my pain, anger, and sadness. Oh, I wish this moment would never pass.*

In March 2012, I received the investigator's report. There was no indication that she had contacted any of my witnesses, only Chaostina and Jane. Once again, there was corruption and systematic racism in the organization. Because of their oppression and prejudices, the blame shifted to me yet again. Once more, the investigator's decisions concluded: "Your actions contributed to a negative work environment and resulted in irreparable damage . . . [You] spoke to the complainant in a condescending/belittling tone. [You] spoke negatively about the complainant to others."

Dear Diary,

The meeting on Thursday, March 22, with the superintendent liaison, the person I conversed with regarding Jane's rage. Unfortunately, the Board disciplined me on Friday, March 23, 2012, and removed me from W.J. Stonesworth to shadow a white Office Administrator. I will learn how to deal with people since I have created a hostile working environment.

The Indian teacher who was lingering in the office was their key witness. They knew what they were planning. Again, this was another setup because I'm Black; it would be a progressive discipline based on Mitsy's allegation.

Even though in 1834, Britain abolished slavery throughout the British Empire, including North America, the legacy of colonialism was still rooted in the Canadian system. A racist belief that Blacks are inferior and whites are superior had become a reality. They did everything to prevent me from being in leadership and ignored my complaints to defend their power.

Jane belittled and tormented me, yet she told

the board's Human Rights and Chaostina that I did the same to her. Chaostina could substantiate her allegations, but my claim was either non-conclusive or unsupported. They used strong language: "condescending tone, treating me like a baby, threatening and that I contributed to a negative or poisonous work environment." The kind of superiority and resentment could only interpret as white privilege.

The common denominator was my race: Jezebella, Mitsy, Jane, and Chaostina were white women. They knew I couldn't challenge their power and privilege. Chaostina ignored my complaints but was the primary witness for Jane. White investigators and administrators existed to protect their race and punished me.

Using nothing but the color of their skin, the clear undertone message they sent me was, we're superior, and we don't want you to give us directions or the face of our schools. Be quiet because you're at the bottom. These behaviors were racist and damaged my reputation and self-esteem.

The union promised me a lawyer because they knew it was unfair. Yet, another empty promise. How could I win? They're white and made the final decision—a partial verdict. To add to my grief, I received a ticket from a cop. He claimed I drove through the stop sign without making a complete stop. Everything is working against me in the moment of my fragility. I was numb. God has given me his divine peace; I'll always be grateful. I may not have the answers, but he's sovereign and has a perfect picture of the situation.

Because of the deceptive scheme, the Board suspended me for one day without pay.

Dear Nadine White:

This letter confirms the details of a disciplinary meeting held on March 22, 2012, to discuss the results of the Workplace Harassment investigation related to complaints originating from W.J. Stonesworth Public School.

Based on the Human Rights Office investigation, we have concluded that your actions again contributed to a hostile work environment and damaged your relationships with the affected staff members. You were reminded that although you were previously provided with a written reprimand and attended coaching counseling, you continue to engage in inappropriate conduct. The following were allegations funded during this latest investigation:

"Nadine (the respondent) spoke to the complainant in a condescending/belittling tone and spoke negatively about the complainant to others.

Given that your actions contributed to a hostile work environment and resulted in the irrevocably damaged working relationship at the school, you are removed permanently from W. J. Stonesworth Public School for the balance of the 2011-2012 school year.

As part of this "work transitioning" process, you will take directions regarding your "work assignment" from the Principal and current Office Administrator of Merebell Junior. If you have any work-related concerns, you should address them with the Principal or seek support from CUPE. Employee Services will provide you with information concerning your placement for the following school year as per the Spring staffing process.

As a result of your actions, you will be suspended for one (1) day on Friday, March 23, 2012, without pay, and we will place a copy of this disciplinary letter in your personnel file. You are again being cautioned that any further incidents or repetition of inappropriate conduct will result in further escalating discipline and will include, but not be limited to, your reassignment to a position with lesser responsibility. You will not be responsible for providing directions to other staff.

After our meeting, we discussed a re-entry plan for your return to work. I also indicated that you do not discuss this matter with anyone as it is confidential. In addition, we expect no reprisal towards anyone who initiated or participated in this investigation, and any action on your part that is retaliatory, directly, or indirectly, will result in further disciplinary action.

Yours truly,

Superintendent of Education

My mouth was dry, and I was breathless. *"God, why me? You have the power to stop it. I can't go through this again. What are you trying to teach me? The ongoing injustice and agony? Nothing makes sense to me anymore."*

On March 26, 2012, I started my new assignment at Merebell Junior. "Lord, I'm asking you for heavenly wisdom, knowledge, and understanding. To continue being humble and keep my tongue under your control."

The cycle of removing and placing me in temporary positions became monotonous. This time was different because I had the added burden of learning lessons from a callous white Office Administrator, Delia. I overheard her blathering with her friends on the telephone. "She's put here because she can't work with other people." *There go the lies, twisted rationale, and breach of confidentiality.*

Three days after I started, Delia said, "I don't know what happened over there, but I'm glad to have you here. What will happen in June? Do you have a choice of where you would want to go?"

"No idea. *It's none of your business. Two-faced.*

I was in a small stuffy library office when I wasn't answering calls, organizing obsolete files, or shredding papers. There were no windows. I didn't lose my momentum. The principal always checked in, ensuring I was doing fine, and encouraged me to sign up for online courses.

That's it, I thought to myself. I need to do it. There were many options, but I chose the ones of my interest. I spent six and a half hours engaging and listening to role plays and scenarios. Despite squinting at the screen's brightness, I enjoyed learning about dealing with difficult people.

I was in the office in the afternoon, and Delia took a sip of water at her desk. "Principals should choose who works in their schools through an interview process. Not speaking to the surplus staff. The Board shouldn't place people in a school without being interviewed because they don't get along with people."

I pressed my lips tightly together, and I kept my expression neutral.

Is this how I should learn to get along with people? Working in an adverse office environment? Like the previous schools I worked in. She was a nightmare, but I stood firm in prayer. "God, deliver me from evil. Restrain Delia's tongue. Stop her from badgering me."

He answered my prayers. Delia's tedious tasks and her insinuations lessened.

The next few days passed busily, which made them feel shorter. It was mid-day, crystal bright, and the kids skipped down the sidewalk. Their laughter sounded as they raced to the corner store for a popsicle. My sandals clicked against the pavement as I turned between the community center and houses from the mid-sixties. I smiled, feeling upbeat.

At last, staffing administrators assigned me a permanent placement at Northarn East Public School in September. I began the position earlier than anticipated.

Chapter 11
Next Act

As I entered the building, chairs were in two rows on either side of the hallway. An artificial plant stood beside the office doorway. One desk rested adjacent to the entrance and another at a window. To the right were the staff mailboxes. The principal and vice-principal offices adjoined.

On tour, I noticed the previous grade eight graduates' photos hanging on the wall—paintings with Black people, Chinese, South Asians, and whites reflecting the rich cultures in the community. Most of the classes were on the first level. The second floor had a learning differences class, a science lab, and a music room.

The school was a revolving door of several short-term Office Administrators and a substitute principal. Employee service had reduced the full-time secretary position to half-time, and then she transferred to another location.

Over the next two weeks before the summer break, I finished the end-of-year responsibilities: created students' schedules and registrations, responded to parents' inquiries, and organized the office for the upcoming school year. I was back in my element, doing what I liked.

Dear Diary,

I'm confident the worst is behind me. It's joyful knowing my life isn't a struggle as before. As I move forward, I walk in God's purpose and will. The freedom to live without guilt and shame is like a precious stone to cherish.

Calvin took me to Red Lobster restaurant for my birthday: I ate buttery, cheesy biscuits, soup, garden salad, shrimp pasta, and an apple pie with vanilla ice cream. For the next couple of days, I slow down my eating.

Giving God thanks for the little and plenty is a way to acknowledge his blessings. He shows his love by using individuals. In this, he's right next to me, celebrating. He's my greatest supporter and always cheering me on.

Thank you, Jehovah, for your blessings. July 20, 2012

Mid-August, I went to Jamaica for a ten-day vacation. More than 90% of Jamaicans identified as Black; the other percentages were comprised of European, Chinese, Indian, and Middle Eastern. English has been the primary language, and every actual Jamaican speaks Patois. In 1962, Jamaica received its independence from Britain and formed a self-government.

My identity and values were tied intrinsically to music and culture. Reggae originated in the late 1960s from Ska: combined with Caribbean mento, calypso, American Jazz, rhythm, and blues. The lyrics, over time, sprung from solid resistance to white culture and domination. Bob Marley's heartfelt message of peace, unity, and religious devotion, *"One Love,"* hit the international stage in 1965. He transformed music from just entertainment to political and racial awareness.

Donald Quarrie, Merlene Ottey, Usain Bolt, and Shelly-Ann Fraser-Pryce were some of our best track and field Olympians. Historically, we challenged ourselves to venture into new territories and persevered amidst criticism. The Island blazed with heat all year round, but we had a bobsled team qualify for the Winter Olympics in 1988. The four men climbed out and pushed to the end, although they didn't finish the event. This story inspired the *Cool Runnings movie* in 1993.

Jamaican voices echoed across the social injustice stage. Bromley Armstrong, Black Civil Rights, and Trade Union Activist, came to Canada in 1947 when he was 19. He became the first Black welder at Massey-Harris Ltd. His passion and mission were focused on promoting African-Canadian rights. He fought for the Fair Employment Practices Act against workplace discrimination and restaurants that refused to serve Blacks.

Marcus Garvey, an influential leader, once said, "The Black skin is not a badge of shame, but rather a glorious symbol of national greatness." He also said, "Emancipate yourself from mental slavery; none, but ourselves, can free our minds." A favorite quote that I repeated to keep me grounded. These words rang aloud in one of Bob Marley's songs.

We loved nature, organic food, natural herbs, spices, fruit punch, and Christmas cake laced with our signature Wray & Nephew white overproof rum.

Returning reminded me of my rich heritage, the foundation that shaped me. My mother taught me many life lessons, but her saying, "Love God and respect others. It's more important than money," I often practiced.

Air Canada landed at Montego Bay Airport at 12:50 p.m. The hot, humid wind slapped against my legs as I pulled my luggage outside. People lined up on the sidewalk, waiting for their transport. In the distance, the car turned and stopped in front of a black Jeep. The rear door opened, and I entered while the driver loaded the luggage in the trunk. I enjoyed the two-hour journey to St. Elizabeth, mesmerized by the mountains and greenery.

Calvin's vacation home had no central air. The sunny days had many outdoor activities; I slept with a standing fan on sultry nights to keep cool.

I stopped to see my auntie; she had no children and was frail with darkened eyesight and dementia. But our family provided her with housing, food, and other essentials.

To my surprise, C.M. was there visiting her father from the USA. She was my best teen friend, and we had grown up living next door to each other. Life got in the way, and we drifted apart for many years. We spent less than an hour reminiscing about our friendship and posed for selfies.

On day four of my trip, I went to Little Ochie,

a seafood restaurant with authentic dishes and a captivating ocean view. I feasted on a medium-sized fish, seasoned with natural spices cooked on the spot, and steamed bammy (made from cassava), my choice of staple, as well as organic pineapple and mango fruit juice blend.

I strode on the dazzling white sand beach, and there was a sudden downpour, but I didn't mind. The raindrops beat on my face and reminded me of my childhood when I played in the rain.

Milk River was my final stop, a spa with warm mineral water flowing from a rock through the blue checkered tub. I waded in the bath for twenty minutes. They said it cured people with rheumatoid arthritis, sciatica, backache, nerve conditions, and liver disorder. My skin got smoother, and the small solid bumps disappeared. After a soothing soak, I indulged in luscious, jerked chicken and cold drinks.

On the way to the airport, a few vans passed, honking to overtake us on a single-lane street. Traffic slowed down when we got into town, and there was intermittent congestion. *Already people are on their way to work*, I thought.

At the airport, I was at a busy departure terminal with passengers checking in. Many travelers waited in line to check in their luggage. I viewed the information screen and saw that Air Canada had canceled my flight. *Is this real? Why didn't anyone contact me?* Others were using curse words.

About forty-five minutes later, an Air Canada customer service agent appeared at the counter. "The flight is canceled due to a storm. We apologize for any inconvenience this may cause. We'll be offering vouchers and a hotel until further notice."

I knew my mom and son were okay, but I was anxious about work.

I rolled my eyes. *Unacceptable. No warning. No communication. If this is because of a storm, why is WestJet leaving for Toronto on time? They're going to the same place. There's more going on here. It might be an engine problem, and they don't want to scare us.*

The sun shone brightly outside as we boarded the tour bus to the hotel. Everyone stood in line when we entered and waited to register at the front desk. After I had collected my key, I went to my room.

Inside was a queen size bed, two-seat sofa, small table, and fridge. I peered through the window, hearing the calming waves and the ocean moving toward the shore. *I didn't pay for this mini-vacation, and I will enjoy it.*

Late mid-afternoon, I hastened to the dining room to eat before closing. Exhausted and hungry, I grabbed some pasta, barbecued chicken, and salad, enough to keep me up until dinner.

Next, I strolled around the grounds, focusing only on the broad ocean and luscious garden. The blue wavey water made me think of God's wondrous creation, his gift to humanity. Hibiscus branches and leaves were deep green, red, and pink; poinciana blooms in yellow and orange. There was beauty everywhere.

A soft wind blew on my back as the sun faded while I returned to my room.

I had a long shower. I dimmed the bathroom light, peeled back the cover, and crawled into bed. Seconds later, I had fallen asleep.

I woke up, brushed my teeth, and went for breakfast in the morning. I grabbed cooked green bananas, ackee and codfish, carrot muffin, hot chocolate, and organic orange juice.

Satisfied, I left the dining area and headed back to my room. I showered, packed my luggage, and checked out before noon. I lounged in the air-conditioned hotel lobby until the large coach rolled in at 2:30 p.m.

Within forty-five minutes, we arrived at the airport. There was no reason to rush because the plane embarked at 2:00 a.m. on Monday, but I was nervous, thinking I might not get to work on time. The time went by quickly while we were sharing stories.

I couldn't call in sick without a doctor's note or take a vacation day because I had none. On the first day back, parents would wait to register their kids for school, but it was too late to worry.

The plane landed just before 6:00 in the morning. I grabbed my luggage and went through immigration in an instant. Calvin stood waiting outside the Air Canada arrival.

I removed a tan blouse from my wardrobe and slid it over my head. I ran downstairs, picked up my lunch, jumped into my car, and rushed to work at eight o'clock.

"Hi, may I speak with the principal?" I said.

"Who are you?"

"I'm the new Office Administrator."

"Oh, I'm Repona, the principal."

"Nice to meet you."

Repona, a tall Jewish woman, wore a light blue and white shirt. She gasped for air when she spoke. She had heart surgery and just returned from medical leave.

"This is your desk." She pointed. It was credenza shaped and adjacent to the entrance—a computer monitor, keyboard below the surface, and telephone with multiple lines to my left. A matching filing cabinet to the right and in the middle was a Public Address (PA) electronic system used for announcements— the cork bulletin board on the wall with yard duty schedules and emergency plans.

"Thank you."

It was a grueling first day after traveling back from Jamaica. I was a zombie walking in daylight and suffering from sleep deprivation. I splashed water in my eyes several times to stay awake.

Leslie, the white half-time afternoon office staff, and I were new to the school. We liked each other immediately, and I hoped we'd get along.

As I set sight on a new normal, the mistreatment was underway within a week and peaked over the next three months. Repona held me responsible for keeping a parent waiting when she told me my workday began at 8:30 a.m.

I walked into the hallway rattled. Martha, an Italian teacher with blonde highlights, sensed something was amiss and motioned me to her classroom. I went, though I didn't know who to trust. Still, her classroom wasn't a regular hang-out for me.

Martha ate blueberries and strawberries from her red Tupperware.

"Sit down, Nadine."

"Thanks."

I sat on the blue kid's chair and glanced at the wall's games, letters, numbers, days, and months charts. A sand table was to the side for children to play.

"Is everything okay, Nadine?"

"Why do you ask?"

"You look a little dazed."

"I don't want to say."

"You can eat with us here anytime. It's a safe place for you."

"Is it OK?"

"Of course." She placed her hands at her sides.

Whenever I was not in my car or walking, I had lunch in her classroom, away from the staffroom and Repona's constant interruptions.

One day, I overheard rumors from two teachers standing by the library doorway.

"The investigator is coming soon."

For once, I was not her primary target, but I knew something had gone wrong because of the high tension in the building. Many staff members avoided the office and lingered in their classrooms. I found myself thinking, *This time, the Board can't blame me for creating a hostile working atmosphere.*

Repona threw tantrums and banged on the beige metal filing cabinet because I forgot to open it. After the superintendent advised her to inform me when she was leaving the building, she yelled, "You must be the one who reported me to my boss. Do you want to know everywhere I'm going?"

"Not at all. None of my business." I moved away from her.

Deep in my heart, she was right. I notified the superintendent before she asked me, but I couldn't admit it because of her fury. If there were any emergencies, I had no information or contacts. It wasn't the first Repona had left the school for over an hour without an administrator.

She followed me to my desk, slamming her fist on the counter, "Answer me . . ."

"Please don't talk to me like this. I'm not your child." I arose from my chair and walked away to phone the union. Reeling from my past, I didn't want history to repeat itself.

Masking the turmoil and terror raging in me, I locked my car and cried out, "God, not again. If she's not willing to change, move her." I had a surge of complete assurance, knowing she would be gone.

In the staffroom, I sat at the redwood table with my right foot crossed over the other. I told a colleague who saw her behavior, "Repona will be leaving."

"How can you tell? We've been praying for five years, and you're here for three months. Does God answer your prayers and not ours?"

"I don't think so."

"But who told you?"

"Gut feeling."

Christmas break was a week away. On my drive to work, Calvin rang me, "Your principal is leaving."

I gripped the steering wheel and shouted, "Is it true?"

"Yes. Repona will be changing schools in January."

"Thank you, God. Please send someone who fears you; loves people and children."

"You'll be okay. Repona's replacement is not a Black but an Asian."

"I'm going to think the best."

"That's all you can do."

I kept thinking, trying to fathom the mystery of God.

Dear Diary,

I'm looking for exciting things to take place. God's favor will multiply with extraordinary blessings and divine intervention. I expect an immense harvest and believe everything will come to fruition.

Isa. 40 says, *Wait upon the Lord, and he'll renew my strength. The everlasting God, the creator of the ends of the earth, faint not, neither is weary, and there is no searching of his understanding.*

Chapter 12
God Answers Prayer

It was cold, but the sun was out. Hannah, Korean and my new boss, wore a brownish long knitted sweater with her hair in a bun. She dropped in at Northarn East after her promotion. She stood at my desk, waiting until I hung up the phone.

"Hi, I'm Nadine, Office Administrator."

"Hannah." We shook hands.

"Did you speak with Repona?"

"Briefly, but she gave me a little information."

S*trange.*

"Here's the checklist. Please check the ones you and Repona discussed. I will fill you in on what wasn't covered."

"Thank you."

There was something about her demeanor that was calming and gracious. I embraced her, a welcoming gesture, and she beamed at me in appreciation.

January 2013 was not only a new year, but we were working with a brand-new principal. I had no problem with professionalism but struggled with trusting people. We collaborated in decision-making, planning, and building teams. I was optimistic about finally getting the appreciation I deserved.

One early afternoon, while I was sitting at my work desk, Calvin phoned. "I'm calling your mom, but she's not answering the telephone."

"She's probably getting ready for her appointment."

"I'm close by."

"If you ring the doorbell and don't hear her, open the door with your key."

"Talk to you."

I hope nothing terrible happens.

"Hello," I answered when Calvin called again shortly after.

Calvin's voice was troubling. "I found your mom sitting in the bathroom. Unconscious."

"Is she okay? Call the ambulance."

"She's not hurt. I'll call you back."

I sat up straighter. My neck and shoulder muscles tensed, and I started breathing heavier and feeling disoriented. My mother has always been a rock and support for me in hard times. She meant the world to me and losing her was unthinkable.

Hannah was on the phone when I went to speak with her. "Excuse me," I said. "I have an emergency. My mother is on her way to the hospital."

"I'm sorry, Nadine. Are you okay? Can you drive yourself?"

"I guess."

"I don't want you to go alone. Wait, I'm coming with you."

"How are you getting back?"

"My husband."

She spoke with the vice-principal, and we hastened to my car.

We arrived at Jay's school in less than an hour. The distance seemed shorter than usual. Hannah assured me, "Your mom is going to be okay." It put my mind at ease.

I made a quick stop at home to collect Mama's clothing.

Oshawa Hospital was within ten minutes. I parked underground.

Jay held my right hand and Hannah stood to my left as we proceeded to the emergency door. I froze. An overwhelming fear struck me.

But Hannah said, "You can do it, Nadine."

I took a short deep breath and stepped inside. Calvin was sitting doing a Sudoku puzzle.

"Hi, Calvin. Please meet my Principal, Hannah."

"I heard so much about you, Calvin."

"Nadine spoke highly of you, Hannah."

They looked at me and laughed with admiration.

"If I were a moment late, your mom would have fallen forward and hit her head on the wall or tile," Calvin said.

"Similar to when she was unresponsive in the past?"

"Yes."

"That would be very serious."

Hannah listened with intent. She peeked at her phone. "Nadine, my family is waiting outside. Take as much time as you need with your mom. We'll talk soon. Calvin, pleasant chatting with you."

"Let me walk with you. Thank you for being so kind and accompanying me," I said.

"My pleasure, Nadine."

The nurse called me inside. "Come with me." She was young and neatly dressed in her burgundy scrub. The faint disinfectant smell made me want to barf. Patients shrieked in pain, and darts pierced my chest.

I followed her to Mama's small room.

"Please wait here. The doctor will speak with you shortly."

Mama was lying with the head of her bed raised at a forty-five-degree angle. The nurse tied the blue-striped hospital gown in the back.

A faint smile crossed her lips when I walked inside. "You come?"

"Yes, Mama. Are you in pain?"

"No. I'm hungry."

"I'll get you home soon."

The doctor said, "Your mom appears to have had a seizure-like episode. Please take her to your family physician for a follow-up with a neurologist."

The next day, I kept Mama company, ensuring her full recovery. Sitting on the floor, watching her slumber, triggered my memory. *Hannah dedicated her time to helping orphans, the elderly, at-risk youths, and volunteering at the children's Christmas breakfast in the community. She was a selfless person. No wonder, without thinking twice, she ensured my safe arrival in the hospital. Her commitment to the success of all students was notable. They were at a disadvantage and frequently ignored by the white prejudiced teachers. But she advocated for support whenever possible.*

That's what it means to be an educator. She had integrity. If it were Repona, she wouldn't care about those things, only the accolades and the physical appearance of the building.

My phone rang, and I answered on the second ring. Calvin asked, "How's your mom feeling today?"

"Much better."

"Tell her I called, and I'll drop by to see her after work."

"For sure."

I was in a perfect bubble until it burst.

Jack, a white science teacher, had a sideways glance. Other than teaching, a few of our administrative roles overlapped because he was the report card administrator. If there were errors, I would give him a copy for corrections. Whenever I handed him the information, I could feel how much he despised a Black woman telling him what to do.

He stood in the office beside my desk. "Show me the site where you get the report," he said.

I logged on. "Please come closer so you can see.

Here it is," and I stepped aside.

"Why can't I have access? Are you telling me how I should do my job?"

Because of his role, the Board didn't permit him to do the reports. I turned around, looked through the glass wall, and fixated on the picture in the hallway, agitated.

The following day, I noticed Jack fumbling through my mailbox. *Is he looking for the toner order he put in there a few days ago?* I watched the time on my computer, and it was 9:15. He walked towards my desk and leaned over. "We need to talk." He gave me an angry stare, repeating the same questions he had asked me a day earlier.

"Am I *annoying* you?" He bobbed his head and shrugged his shoulder.

"You're not," I said, and I left immediately.

In a meeting with Hannah and Jack, I read my notes verbatim. "Returning the second time, accusing me clearly indicated contempt. It saddens me as we should treat each other with respect and dignity. I was distressed and lost my appetite. I could consider this kind of behavior harassment. Sometimes I find it difficult to communicate with you. You're getting defensive. I'm walking on eggshells. My work ethic, everything is being questioned and monitored."

His nostrils flared, and his legs shook. There was a brief silence before Hannah asked him to respond. Jack remained quiet until I exited the room. After that, he sent email messages and copied Hannah, which relieved me from further antagonizing and insults.

Six weeks later, Violet, the French teacher, was standing behind me, awaiting my attention, hair braided in two and her black skin flawless. Afterward, she took a few steps forward to greet me after I finished speaking to a parent.

"Hi Nadine, a busy day."

"A rather interesting morning."

"I've something to share with you."

"I'm listening."

"You taught us budget procedures, and Ontario student records ministry guidelines. "Why don't you become a teacher? Teaching adults."

"A fantastic idea! But where do I get the information? I thought of this many times, and my doctor encouraged me."

"I'll send it to you."

"You're awesome! Another thing, I'm interested in doing a conflict resolution course. Can you help me?"

"Let me do some research and email it to you as well."

The stars are aligning. I searched for these programs for a while but had no luck. And now opportunities are knocking at my door.

She sent the link download to the course summary in an email.

The fall 2013 semester began for the online Adult Education at Brock University. It was a four-year program, but they awarded me credits for my first three years since I had a previous degree. My spirit flew high, and my feet barely touched the ground. "I did it again, Mama. Only five courses."

Mama was in the kitchen at home, prepping for dinner. She took the Montego mild curry powder, black pepper, salt, and mixed spices from the cupboard, add to the chicken pieces, and rubbed them with her bare hands. Her brown eyes twinkled. "I'm happy for you."

In the late afternoon of June 13, 2014, I drove 10-20 kilometers in bumper-to-bumper traffic. I turned the handle, so the window went down, and the heat blew in. With a sudden jerk, the car moved forward and backward; my head moved and jolted forward; and back again. I opened the door in seconds, jumped out of my car, and shouted at the driver. "What were you doing? What's wrong with you?"

He looked at me with a blank stare.

I returned inside and drove to a side street. My head drooped backward on the headrest from a sudden spell of dizziness, headache, and weakness. It took my brain a few seconds to stabilize. I pressed my vehicle's "On Star" button; police, ambulance, and fire came to the scene. The paramedics put me on a stretcher and drove me to the hospital.

I remember the attending physician saying, "You'll be in a lot of pain. Take the medication I prescribed and see your family doctor."

In September 2014, I returned to work, although I could not sit for more than twenty minutes due to excruciating lower back pain. I couldn't take time off because I had to support my mom and son. It wouldn't cover all my expenses even if I received insurance payments.

One day, I forgot where to turn and smacked my mouth on the bathroom wall. "It's okay, Nadine," Hannah told me when I showed her my lip.

But the next day, it was puffy and painful. She said, "That's a nasty bruise."

"Why didn't you tell me yesterday?"

"Because I knew you would feel bad."

The first day following the Christmas break, I stepped out of bed, and my feet landed on the taupe color carpet. I could barely stand up without holding on to the dresser. I gripped the handrail slowly down the stairs, bending forward into the kitchen.

"What's wrong?" Mama asked.

"I'm not sure. I need to see the doctor."

"Try to get in before Christmas."

"Yes, Mama."

Dr. Long examined me and read the CT scan results done a month before. "You have bulging discs in your lower back. Continue with the physiotherapy treatment."

I slumped in my car. *Why didn't he let me know when he got the results?*

I worked four hours in the mornings until the end of February, frequently alternating between sitting and standing. It now took me twenty to thirty minutes to complete the tasks. I was easily distracted and took a long time to process and recall information. I lurched with a cane. Sometimes, I rested on four chairs during breaks in a quiet room.

Hannah was supportive. Yet when I thought of Jezebella, Mitsy, Jane, and the horrible administrators, I remembered the horrific experiences. Every interaction and action with the secretary amplified my fear of losing my job. My poor work performance and inability to keep up with my responsibilities were frightening. I screamed in agony when the emotional and physical pain became too severe.

On March 17, 2015, the pain specialist inserted a long needle in my back with a cortisone shot. The injection was to reduce inflammation and speed up the healing process. Initially, I had little or no pain. However, the second and last doses were excruciating.

Learning to walk again was a chore. I started with baby steps on the treadmill and strengthening exercises with light weights at the physio. Sorrow swept over me.

In May, I began pain management therapy with a psychologist once every two weeks. Dr. K wore a white shirt with dark jeans when we first met. We chatted about the accident and its effect. At the end of each session, I had a twenty-minute relaxation with deep breathing. The lights were out, and I closed my eyes while on my back. I was fidgeting and restless but snoozed after I was comfortable.

Before the accident, I had a retentive memory, but notepads and calendars had become a part of my daily routine so I could remember things.

In one of my sessions with Dr. K., he said, "Nadine, the stress on your brain is causing your memory loss."

"There's no tension in my shoulder or neck."

"Your stress is being manifested in your brain."

"How do I get my memory back?"

"Retraining your memory."

"How?"

"In addition to relaxation, try to learn something new."

Meanwhile, I struggled with my last course but graduated with a Bachelor of Adult Education, with distinction, on June 10, 2015. I attained a Dispute Resolution Certificate in July at York University, a one-month accelerated course. My memory was still a challenge, but I received steady accommodations from professors, extended time to complete assignments and options for final exams.

In September, Hannah transferred to a middle school.

Chapter 13
The Replacement

Hannah prepared me for her departure, so it wasn't a surprise. Yet a bit of uncertainty and anxiety permeated my thoughts. Not knowing much about the replacement and losing her propelled me to apply for job postings, hoping for a new environment.

"You're leaving for the wrong reasons," Hannah told me.

I agreed. I knew I had to learn to accept changes made by myself or someone else. I was too tired and afraid of the unknown and got a sign that God had another plan after two unsuccessful interviews. I was still figuring out His road map for my life. Sometimes I grew impatient, but it was okay because He would reveal everything at the right time.

Over the summer break, I browsed through the college catalog. *I could start studying English again and teaching English as a Second Language—linguistics, culture, and grammar. This was new knowledge and for sure will retrain my memory.*

I recalled the neurologist's questions: "What grade education do you have?" I couldn't identify or match simple pictures. In his final report, he wrote, "*She has significant problems in visual-spatial, executive, and delayed recall measures.*"

I'd do anything to get back my cognitive ability. It's a Black woman's power.

Charlton was the new principal and a white Canadian. He gazed into space and seemed confused all the time. I waited for a couple of weeks for him to adjust. I asked him, "Do you have a moment to discuss office expectations?"

"Continue what you always did in the past." He made no eye contact but let me talk while he walked ahead. Or, he would say, "I'm busy."

He did some of my administrative tasks and asked other teachers to do them. Those duties were part of my job description, but he didn't want to speak with me. For three years and six months, I'd had some dignity. Communication and respect were the basis of our office. Now, the toxicity from Repona's history reappeared.

Elizabeth, a white teacher who wore turquoise earrings, strolled into the office on Tuesday morning and cleared her throat. "Are you okay?" She came closer and held me. My watery eyes filled with worried. "I miss Hannah."

"Me too." There were fewer connections, less respect, and favoritism abounded after Hannah's transfer.

The snow fell, tiny specs of ice floating on our forehead while Elizabeth and I strolled into Starbucks, our favorite lunch hangout, to sip Frappuccino. She became my close friend. I still struggled with trust issues but could talk with her about my personal and work life.

"What are you staring at?" I asked one day.

Elizabeth laughed, "Eye candy."

"He's cute."

"That's what I'm thinking."

"How about you? Anyone lately?"

"You know, these guys don't want commitment," I said. "They have no idea what they want. If you're confident, they feel threatened. A woman who texts or calls a lot, she's needy. But I'm not selling myself short. The right one will come along."

"Absolutely! I don't want a man who doesn't work, and I don't want a player."

I nodded in agreement.

"It's time to go back."

Elizabeth was promoted to another school Board, and my trips to Starbucks stopped.

In my car, while trying to relax, sometimes I found my thoughts drifting to staff members' racism and arrogance. Lona, a short, grey-haired, white woman whose office was a few doors down from mine, would say, "I can hear you in my classroom." Or "You have baggage" when she refused to share a vacant office I could use to work on time-sensitive tasks. Her insulting statements denoted a racial undertone.

Bilha, a Jewish teacher, flashed her hand across my face while I was speaking to another staff member.

Gayran was South Asian, tall, and walked with a limp. He screamed at me in rage and blamed me for his lack of work ethic. Hannah dealt with him before he went to China to teach for three years. Now he was back and started up where he had left off.

"Stop now," I said firmly.

But Charlton, my boss, blasted me. "Your actions are inappropriate in the office." Still, he never did any investigation. He never tried to deal with harassment until matters spiraled out of control. I thumped into the photocopier room with watery eyes.

Maria asked, "What's wrong?"

"I despise Gayran." The hate for him was what I had felt for Jezebella all those years ago. I had come so far, and yet so little had changed.

I was heartbroken and sick from persistent punishments and attacks. Then the COVID-19 pandemic in 2020 happened, a pivotal time in history when the planet joined forces to fight against anti-Black racism.

Chapter 14
My Identity

Systematic racism was entrenched in the normative structure of the Greater Toronto Area School Board and the City of Toronto, oppressing Black people. Throughout history, the hostility and manipulation of dominant groups fabricated their stories to destroy and diminish my voice and the voices of other Black people. But 2020 was a year of global anti-Black racism revelation. Amy Cooper, a white Canadian, told harmful lies about a Black man; the Minnesota police officer knelt on a Black man's neck until he died, and both situations generated conversations throughout mainstream social media networks.

In the first instance, Amy Cooper walked her unleashed dog in Central Park, New York, contrary to the rule. Christian, a Black man, politely asked her to keep her dog on a leash. She told him, "I'm going to call the police."

"Please tell them whatever you like," said Christian.

She phoned the police. "There's an African American man who has a bicycle helmet. He's recording me and threatening my dog and me. A man is threatening me. Please send the cops immediately."

In the second, I watched the video and heard

George Floyd's voice as he wailed while the officers tortured him. "My stomach hurts, my neck hurts. I can't breathe." Finally, his motionless body lay on the ground. The crowd begged them to stop, but they disregarded their pleas.

Following these cases and after hearing the plight of racial discrimination against Blacks, I sat in my car, paralyzed, and traumatized. I relived similar experiences from start to finish. An inner urge to scream subsumed my shock and grief.

Milley, a Jewish teacher, was tall and had a bulging belly. I diligently met her relentless demands, knowing she would hassle me. Her emails had the same questions she just asked me but with different wording. If Milley didn't receive the expected answers, she would make her way to the office to see me.

In November 2019, Milley approached me during a hectic morning. "Nadine, do you know when I will be receiving my supplies?"

"You should be getting them soon."

"Did you place my order?"

"Yes, I did."

Minutes after she left the office, I saw her email. "Nadine, if you did not place my order, please replace it with this one . . ."

I went to Charlton. "I'm confused," I said. "I had the exact conversation with Milley before she sent me this email. I'm uncertain how to respond."

He shook his head, side to side. "I don't understand

either."

Milley walked in the following mid-morning when all the phone lines were ringing, and I was trying to catch up on my emails. "Nadine, can I ask you a question?"

"Sure, go ahead."

"You don't answer your email?"

"Yes, I do."

"So, why didn't you reply to the one I sent you?"

I took a deep long gulp of air, "I answered your question yesterday."

She bent over my desk towards me, "You didn't. You ignored my email."

"Well, I've answered all your questions, and you kept coming at me. I want you to stop; this behavior could be considered harassment."

"I'm going to tell Charlton that you call me a racist."

"Go ahead."

She shouted his name. "Charlton!" But he stepped into the hallway.

Her constant microaggressions and offensive attitude over the years became an emotional ruin. Days turned into weeks, yet I never heard anything about her claim that I called her a racist. The holiday came and went. We were back in school in January 2020, but in February, while I was going home from an offsite workshop, Charlton phoned me. "Hi, Nadine. How was your workshop?"

"It was informational." I got the impression there was something more than a pleasant call. My gut wrenched, making me feel nauseous.

"You have a meeting on Friday with your union."

"What's the reason?"

"An incident with a staff member."

"When was this?"

"I can't say anymore."

It wasn't fair. Charlton was mindful of Milley's conduct but remained quiet and waited for the perfect moment to blame me for her actions. There had been too many escalations to employee services. Too many abuses. Too many allegations. Too much silencing.

Milley retaliated because I called her out, accusing me of calling her a racist. The Board was least interested in hearing my position and threatened punitive action.

"Did you call Milley a racist . . . ?" Charlton asked me repeatedly.

"I have something to say. It had been a long-standing problem, but you ignored my many complaints. You didn't speak with me before escalating it to employee services."

He continued, evading my statement. "Did you call Milley a racist?"

"No."

He left to speak with employee services. When he came back, he gave me a verbal warning. Despite my reply, their actions upheld narcissism, aligned with white power and privileges. Speaking the correct language and knowing the "code" permitted them to disguise their harmful behavior toward me.

Everything I had suffered became crystal clear. The playbook had been bait, gaslighting to get my reactions and destroy my self-esteem. Middle Eastern, East, and South Asians knew the language—those anti-Black minority groups emulated their oppressors. I didn't understand what I was doing wrong all those years. I did everything I was supposed to, going to work, and going through the proper channels. Still, none worked because the organizational policies and procedures perpetuated my disadvantages.

Our Black boys and girls suffered chronic stress from some of our Asian and white teachers. One Asian teacher described a grade one Black kid as "A big Black boy hurting the small kids (white and Asian)." Or I heard her tell a grade two Canadian-born Black boy, "I don't understand what you're saying," insinuating he fibbed after the kid told me he fell and hit his head in her classroom.

Most white teachers granted grace to the impolite and defiant white students. But if a Black student did something similar or less, they removed them from the class.

That's it, I thought to myself. I will no longer allow anyone to flash hands across my face, yell at me, muzzle my mouth, or blame me for their toxicity and actions.

A long history of inequitable, degrading laws and policies only exacerbated the problem of white privilege. The whites built them into the core of our labour and educational system as the foundation for structural racism——entrenched and intertwined with diminishing my voice to complete silence.

Years passed, but it seemed like yesterday, and the pain was still raw. Irrespective of the obstacles, I decided I would no longer conceal my authentic identity but would cut through others' delusions. After all, it hadn't always been this way.

On a warm summer's morning in July, a beautiful baby girl swooshed her way into a peculiar world, cradled and loved by her mother and father.

I was born on the Island of Jamaica, with white sand beaches and majestic waterfalls. African, European, East Indian, and Chinese heritage shaped my cultural individualism. I had a religious belief rooted in the Pentecostal tradition, the freedom to have ambition, equality, independence, and success. Economic stability and emotional support were the underpinning cultures of my family unit.

Many individuals used their shortcomings and fears to damage me, but I denied their insidious imagery, actions, and cynicism. I do not need anyone's approval to illuminate my light. I am elegant, tall, brown-eyed, dark with toned skin, and an infectious laugh.

Most people tend to focus on their pitfalls, but I magnified resilience and fearlessness. In the pit of rejection, I became shrewder; encircled myself with positive influences.

Sometimes I wonder, "Who am I?" I realized my

survival in no way depended on affluence, economy, or earthling relationships, but on Christ. Paul, the apostle in the bible, spoke of my true ideals. *God blessed me with spiritual gifts. I am blameless in His sight, forgiven, and extraordinary (Eph. 1).*

My inadequacies never reversed the opinions of God. He favored and loved me. His plans were more than I envisioned. *"For I know the thoughts toward you, peace, and not evil and to show an expected end" (Jer. 11).* God's standards constructed my unique individuality. I am not a replica of mortals' ideology, failures, and frailty.

I buried this secret inside me, the power to advocate for change. I drew on events to reshape my consciousness of how I perceived myself and to transform my destiny.

Chapter 15
Moving Forward

The pandemic shone a bright light on hatred and anti-Black racism as something that had been going on for many centuries. The murder of George Floyd and Amy Cooper's falsity unveiled the unending disparities on the planet.

Canadian society prohibited hate crimes, racist jokes, and slurs, while other schemes appeared acceptable. For over twenty-five years, I shouldered the persecutors' tone monitoring, victim-blaming, voice muzzling, and complaints to law enforcement and persons in authority.

In retrospect, I had made many strides to improve my life: I obtained certificates in dispute resolution, became a certified English language teacher, and received a mediation designation. In addition, I worked during my accident, doing spiritual cleansing and emotional healing therapy sessions to help me deal with my feelings and stressors. The gained experiences and knowledge allowed me to empower individuals in my sphere of influence.

I envisioned a world of inclusiveness and impartiality. Being assertive was daunting, but suppressing my voice was not an option.

A former School Board Director tweeted, "We

need to work together to choose a stand against individual and systematic acts of anti-Black racism . . . Silence isn't acceptable."

When I saw his tweet, I had just eaten a ripe banana and relaxed in the chair with nothing else to do. It was the perfect opportunity for me to pronounce, "More to do at the school level and employee services . . . We're still without a voice when we're victims of discrimination and other forms of racism. They often punished us on all levels."

"We agree the structure of our system causes silence and harm." He responded.

The power of speech affected change and brought awareness to the universe. Winning the battle of suppression is essential. Otherwise, those who come after me might do as I did, internalize pain, and collapse under fear.

Following George Floyd's death on June 5, 2020, I watched the anti-Black racism protest on the CTV network on Parliament Hill, Ottawa, Canada. I wondered. *How do I address the injustices?*

Meanwhile, the Ministry of Health forced school boards to execute guidelines and strategies to protect their staff from COVID-19, only cohorts to decrease exposures and enable contact tracing.

Before the return of students and staff, I queried, "Charlton, do you have any idea when we're going to put things in place to limit the traffic in the office?" I was worried about my health issues and my mother's well-being because I had to visit her in the nursing home.

"I'm waiting on the Board."

"Other schools have taken action, and we've been waiting for almost two weeks."

"Don't raise your voice. Watch your tone."

I turned in my chair, heart-pounding, "Those comments are so anti-Black."

"Are you calling me a racist?" He shut his door.

These words sent shockwaves through my brain, but I felt empowered. For once, I confronted the years of victim-blaming and scapegoating. In those seconds, I reclaimed my dignity and voice. Charlton pretended to be oblivious to ill-treatment and often faulted me for others' discriminatory actions.

An hour later, he emerged and said, "Nadine, may I speak with you?"

"Absolutely."

"The custodian ordered the shield for your desk. Is there anything else you would like in the office?"

"Can we go over the policy and take it from there?"

"Yes."

Finally, collaboration in executing the Board's directives to protect everyone became a priority.

Yafita, a Middle Eastern secretary, continually interrupted me while I was engrossed in my work and repeated the same questions.

"Nadine, can you help me?"

"One moment."

"Come."

She was seated at her desk at the window, the view looking over the kindergarten play area outside. She fixed her eyes on the computer screen, frantic. "I can't print the document. I'm leaving at 4:00 p.m. It's now 3:30. I have no time to print the labels."

I strode over to her computer and clicked the print button without speaking.

She opened her mouth, eyes lit up, "I thank you. I like working here with you."

"You're welcome."

She returned to work after a day's absence.

I asked, "How are you doing today?"

"My chest pains."

"I'm sorry to hear."

"You know, I'm not happy here."

"But you told me you were happy working at the school two days ago. I don't understand."

"You gave me anxiety."

"No, not this time. I'm not taking on this problem. It's a stressful time for all with constant Covid protocol changes."

Yafita often perpetuated false accusations. But this time was different. We were in the middle of an anti-Black racism movement, and management was prudent—an ideal opening and timing to address racial undertones and biases.

Seconds later, I spoke with Charlton, who suggested a meeting after my break. My teeth clamped together, and I hurried outside for fresh air.

In the meeting, Yafita said, "Nadine is treating me like a baby."

Charlton probed. "What do you mean?"

"Her tone . . ."

"Stop. Everyone blamed Black people for their tone. I had to do some reflections as well," said Charlton.

"Muslims are discriminated against too."

"Yes, I understand, but we're here to discuss current concerns."

"Is there anything else?"

"Nadine is my friend . . ."

"No. We're colleagues." *I'm not playing your games anymore.*

How could she be a friend? My friends were respectful, caring, and trusting. Besides, she was fake and deceitful. She gossiped and bore false tales, causing me harm.

I left the meeting disturbed. Black people were and still are considered at the bottom of society. People of all races compare themselves to us as means of elevating themselves. Cruelty and injustices against Blacks are normalized, blamed, and punished to maintain their social status.

It's an absolute shame for one race to need a "Black Lives Matter" movement, a battle of endless advocacy for justice that's often infuriating.

For me, the future is to take full ownership of my uniqueness and be bold, stopping the brutal cycle of racism.

Chapter 16
Reflection

Would it be such a bad thing to live and work in spaces of equality? In a world free from alienation and scrutiny? Not for days, a few months, or years but a lifetime. Is it insane to think we can escape centuries of cruelty and segregation with no greater purpose than to embrace diversity?

Yes, it can happen. A change in structural policies and universal white supremacy philosophy is necessary to eradicate the barriers of biases, stigma, and disenfranchisement. Individuals need to retrain their minds and unite against anti-Black racism.

How I responded in the face of adversity was vital; either I became bitter or better. *Finding My Voice: Standing Against Racism* is to inspire others to speak their truth, knowing that at last, I gained enough courage to insist upon the voice the City of Toronto and Greater Toronto Area School Board silenced for years.

I can control the effects and benefits in any situation, but not the pain inflicted by others. My wisdom and growth came from life's immense pressures and brokenness. Instead of asking why bad things happen to me, I consoled myself by asking what I could learn from each new crisis.

The story was emotionally challenging to write but empowering, giving me strength with greater hope. Resiliency and faith in God were the secrets to surviving the wilderness and darkest nights. If I failed, I got up and kept trying until I succeeded.

I can now breathe. Open the window and roar like no one is listening just because I am free.

Acknowledgments

To Estelle Laure: thank you for believing I'm a writer.

My friend: Sandra Brown, thanks for your friendship and support. Julie Scott for the book title, excellent advice, and allyship. Heather Walker, always there cheering me on; beta reader and friend; Alicia Anderson, for standing by me over the years; Judith Clarke, who gave me the courage to believe in greatness.

My family: Cousin Karen Maragh; Son Jahson Samuels-Goffe, for your constant support.

Thanks to my health professionals and anyone else who supported me.

In every part of my journey, I remained true to my identity.

About the Author

Nadine White, the author of the forthcoming memoir, *Surviving In A Nursing Home: The Reality of Life Behind the Scenes*, believes in authenticity, integrity, and forgiveness. She is a mediator with many experiences empowering others to deal with difficult situations. Her picture books include *Baby Bunny's Amazing Adventure, Penniboy: A Bratty Bunny, and Penniboy Goes To School,* illustrated by Alyssa Lasko. Nadine has a post-bachelor Certificate in Dispute Resolution from York University, a Q. Med designation from the Alternate Dispute Resolution Institute of Ontario (ADRIO), a Bachelor of Business Administration from York University, and a Bachelor of Adult Education from Brock University. She lives in Ontario, Canada, with her family. Visit Nadine at nadinewhitemediation.com and on Instagram at nadine.white.357.

www.ingramcontent.com/pod-product-compliance
Lightning Source LLC
Chambersburg PA
CBHW071351080526
44587CB00017B/3052